BEYOND *the* BARON

A personal glance at Coach Adolph Rupp

by

Dr. V.A. Jackson

Team Physician

Also VIP Recipes
by

Marie Jackson

McClanahan
Publishing House

International Standard Book Number 0-913383 57 0
Library of Congress Catalog Card Number 97 69850

Recipes used with permission from *Meditations & Menus, Athletes' Recipes* compiled by Marie H. Jackson

Cover design and book layout by James Asher Graphics

Manufactured in the United States of America

All book order correspondence should be addressed to:

McClanahan Publishing House, Inc.
P. O. Box 100
Kuttawa, KY 42055
(502) 388-9388
1-800-544-6959

McClanahan
Publishing House

Other books by McClanahan Publishing House, Inc.

A Little Touch of Grace
Assassination at the State House
Castle: The Story of a Kentucky Prison
Children of Promise
Cincinnati: Specialties of the House
Cunningham Family Cookbook
Dining in Historic Kentucky
Especially Herbs
Flames in the Wind
Kentucky: Dining by the Lakes
Kentucky Keepsakes: Classic Southern Recipes
Ky. College Basketball NAMES & GAMES
Merry Christmas From Kentucky
Miss Patti's Cook Book
Nuts About Pecans
Ohio: The Pleasures and Treasures of Warren County
On Bended Knees: The Night Rider Story
Simply Tennessee
Still Crazy About the Cats
Teacher, Teacher Did You Know...
Whitehaven: The Rebirth of a Southern Mansion

www.kybooks.com

DEDICATION

To my wife, Marie, my daughter, Donna and to all the players and coaches I worked with as U.K. Team Physician, I lovingly dedicate this book.

FRIENDSHIP is a GOLDEN CHAIN,
The links are friends so dear——

And the GOLDEN CHAIN OF FRIENDSHIP
Is a strong and blessed tie,
Binding kindred hearts together
As the years go passing by.

INTRODUCTION BY MRS. JACKSON

A remarkable life of a kind and gentle man began on March 26, 1903. Dr. V.A. Jackson was kind enough to have been a loving husband, father, and grandfather. Also he was kind enough to have provided service to thousands of patients, saved many lives, and delivered hundreds of babies. He was gentle enough to be a team physician for the University of Kentucky Wildcat basketball team for 17 years and be a father figure to all of the players. A man, known as "Papa" by his family and as "Doc" by his patients and friends now rests at his family plot in a beautiful small cemetery in Clinton, KY. At his grave the breeze whispers and the sound of a passing train can be heard in the distance. We are all grateful for having known him and for all he has taught us. His journey of 93 years and 11 months is a testament to the quote in his autobiography: "Dare to dream, be a friend to man and put your trust in God. Only then can your life be successful."

Due to the extended illness of the author, Dr. Jackson was unable to have this remarkable book published before his death. His family thought it only fitting to have it made available to all their many friends because of the beautiful friendship these two great men shared for many years.

The family wishes to thank all those who share in this sincere tribute to our loved one, *our Papa!*

Marie Jackson; Jim and Donna Jackson Vick;
Steve, Leslie and DylanVick; Alan Vick

Whenen Mrs. Jackson approached me about writing this introduction for "Beyond the Baron" I can't explain how excited I was. Not because I get to display my writing abilities, since I am a former athlete not a writer, but because I am eager with anticipation to read the book you now hold in your hands.

You will never find a bigger Kentucky Basketball fan than Dr. V.A. Jackson. The first part of that sentence is used a lot to describe many Kentucky fans, but for "Doc," as all the players know him, his perspective is unique. Doc never played or coached at UK (although he may have had a few suggestions) but he still had an inside view of all the "goings on" with the program over a 17 year period.

Not only was Dr. Jackson the team doctor but many times he was a father figure for a player or a sounding board for a coach. Whether it was a B-12 shot or just someone to talk to, Doc always had time and a friendly smile. To show just how loyal and supportive the Jacksons were, Doc even managed to talk his bride, Marie, into giving up their home so they could move into Wildcat Lodge as the first official house parents. Whether it was during basketball season or trips to Australia and Japan in the off season, Dr. Jackson was always there.

Yes, Dr. V.A. and Marie are true Big Blue fans like no others. Thanks for everything, Doc!!!

Kyle May

Table of Contents

ACKNOWLEDGEMENTS

Life has been so good to me, probably much better than I deserve. In my wonderful home I have been blessed with a precious wife, daughter, two grandsons and a great grandson. I want to thank them for enduring and understanding my love for Kentucky Basketball.

To Marie, my wife, for leaving you alone many, many weekends to be with the team;

To Donna, my daughter, for missing your high school basketball games where you were cheerleader and high school majorette;

To Steve and Alan, my grandsons, for always being late for Christmas because of U.K.I.T. Tournaments every year;

To Dylan, my great grandson, who came along too late to realize my deep love for the sport of Kentucky basketball but tried to get excited when I would tell him basketball stories;

To all the coaches, athletic directors, fans and the University of Kentucky who allowed me to be part of such a wonderful tradition in Kentucky;

Last, but not least, to God for keeping me healthy and allowing me the knowledge to take care of these wonderful young men;

I shall be eternally grateful to all of these, because my life has been truly something beautiful because of the sacrifice of my loved ones. May God care and grant them the joy and fullness of life they so deserve.

To all of these I give thanks, because without them this book would be impossible.

Respectfully,

PREFACE

It has been my honor and pleasure to be Coach Rupp's team physcian the last seven years he coached and his personal physician the last eleven years he lived, so I probably knew the man about as well as anyone outside his immediate family.

To start with, let me say that Adolph Rupp was very different from any man I have ever known. With a unique personality and mannerism, he was highly intelligent - one of the smartest individuals I have ever known. He was a tough, overbearing person and, until you knew him, was quite hard to deal with or even get along with. He was gruff, mean, hard-hearted, soft-hearted, compassionate, affectionate, cooperative, stubborn, and impatient, a proud man, both aloof and friendly. He was a master psychologist which I am sure was one big reason he was such a great coach. He seemed to always know just what to say to a player and how to say it in order to make the player try harder. Some players hated him, others loved him and all of them had a profound respect for him as a man and his ability as a coach. He believed in God but was not afraid of the devil. He was a poor loser but never let losing affect his mannerism. He was an astute businessman and he was brutally honest. He was a stickler for minute details and often told his players, "It's the little things that get you beat." He firmly believed that habits formed in practice were also used in the game, so he was a very strict disciplinarian in practice as well as during a game. Needless to say, his practice sessions were conducted as if they were playing, and practice was a pleasure to watch. Adolph was such a serious-minded man that he had very little time for frivolity and tolerated none during practice from players, coaches or visitors.

Coach Rupp was a man of high morals and ideals, a family man and a gentleman in every respect. I have never known him to say or do anything that might embarrass any lady who might be present.

Inside of his gruff exterior was a big, soft heart that showed only occasionally. During our practice the day before a game in Florida, a janitor's wife and little child sauntered into the gym and Coach Rupp saw them. He left practice immediately and went over and squatted down beside the child and started a conversation with her. Both mother and child became relaxed and were no longer embarrassed.

As a number of people know, the night before a "road" game, there was usually a little stag party in a hotel room, either in my room or Coach Rupp's. I shall long remember one party in Baton Rouge the night before an LSU game. As usual, Adolph visited the bathroom and when he came out, he looked us over and said, "I've got something to tell you bastards. When I die, I want my pallbearers to come from this crowd here - and I don't want a lot of mourning, or acts of sadness going on. When you start to the cemetery with me, I want you to have a fifth of bourbon and enjoy that trip."

Happy Chandler said, "Adolph do you want us to drink that bourbon going to the cemetery or coming back?"

"Hell Happy, you drink it going to the cemetery. I won't be with you coming back."

Happy and I were in the same funeral car the day of the funeral and we reminisced about Adolph's statement that night in the hotel. However, his funeral was a sad occasion indeed and, there was no thought of frivolity whatsoever.

Chapter I

To write about being the personal physician and confidant of such a great and renown man as Coach Adolph Frederick Rupp is no small task. In fact, it is an undertaking of such magnitude that I hardly know how to start.

My first time to ever see the man was a Sunday afternoon in the spring of 1930. Forest "Aggie" Sale and I were leaving the Kentucky Theatre on East Main Street in Lexington, Kentucky, and saw the Coach and Mrs. Rupp coming in. Aggie called out, "Hello Adolph." Coach Rupp answered, "Hello boys. How is the show?" I thought then that a new coach who reacts that way to being called by his first name by one of his players must be a pretty nice gentleman. At that point, he had not started coaching here yet. That incident undoubtedly helped me to form an early opinion or Coach Rupp.

Adolph Rupp was born in Halstead, Kansas, September 2, 1901 of parents who had immigrated from Germany. He was quite proud of his Prussian-German heritage and reminded me of that more than once.

Adolph was raised on a farm not far from Halstead and used to enjoy telling some pretty wild tales relating the hardships the family endured during his childhood. One of his favorite stories concerned how he had to hunt jackrabbits in the snow so his mother would have meat to put on the table.

Strangely, Adolph never mentioned that the family ever had a shortage of bread, cookies or other pastries. Perhaps he was aware of the fact that his listeners were well acquainted with the great wheat fields of Kansas and a shortage of flour was unheard of in that part of the country. But he did tell about how he and his brothers used barrel hoops for baskets and a sack half filled with sawdust or straw for the basketball.

After finishing elementary and high school, Adolph enrolled in Kansas University and played college basketball under the great Coach "Fog" Allen. At that time, Dr. Naismith, the man who invented the game of basketball, was on the faculty at Kansas. So there is good reason that young Rupp received the best coaching available at that time. There is good evidence that he was the number six man on the squad which could also have been a factor in his later becoming such a fantastic basketball coach. In many cases, substitutes have become better coaches than did the big stars.

Basketball scholarships were unknown during this time and one of Adolph's favorite stories was telling of the awful hardships he endured while "working his way through college." I did the same thing during my college days as a pre-med student at the University of Kentucky, but my hardships paled in comparisons to coach Rupp's.

Being a possessor of great wit and humor, Adolph was not one most of us wanted to argue the point with. However in my case, there was one exception. We frequently "crossed swords" over the effects nicotine had on the lungs and he dearly enjoyed these confrontations. Although he never let it appear that I was a winner, I always felt that he agreed with me 100% but admitting so would have killed the show.

After first seeing Coach Rupp that Sunday at the Kentucky Theatre in 1930, I saw very little of him the next couple of years.

I returned to UK in the fall of 1931, after a year of teaching in Harlan High School, for a year of graduate work. During the early summer of 1932, I was appointed principal of the Glasgow High School. That was about the time the Basketball Rules Committee discontinued the use of center-jumps after each basket scored.

Since our high school coach had never seen a game played under the new rule, he was at a loss as how to coach an offense with such a system. So he asked me if I thought Coach Rupp would help us. I wrote the coach and he immediately sent us a set of offensive plays and patterns he had developed for UK and felt sure they could be used in high school. Again, Coach Rupp had acted like a truly big man.

Needless to say, I followed Coach Rupp's and University of Kentucky's basketball games in the sports pages almost daily after that. However, there were no tickets available in Alumni Gym (seating capacity of 3500), hence no way for me to watch his games. So there was a span of several years when our paths seldom crossed.

The Southeastern Conference was formed prior to the 1932 - 33 season. Charter members were Kentucky, Georgia, Georgia Tech, Alabama, Alabama Polytech (now Auburn), Mississippi, Mississippi State, Louisiana State, Tulane, Tennessee, Sewanee, Vanderbilt and Florida.

I remember well seeing the coach on a train some years later. Tennessee had defeated us in the final game of the SEC tournament in Louisville on March 2, 1941. I was a senior in medical school that year and saw that tournament. As I now look back, that "train visit" was probably the real beginning of our lasting friendship. He apparently sensed that he had a sympathetic "audience" and seemed glad to rehash the tournament with me. Among other things, our center James King suffered a fractured leg in the semi-final game the day before against Alabama - otherwise, we both agreed, the Volunteers never would have won that game.

The following year, 1942, after finishing my surgical residency at Kentucky Baptist Hospital, plus two or three months residency at Sampson Community Hospital in Glasgow, Kentucky, I entered the US Army as a Captain, M.C., on September 9. After that I saw Coach Rupp only a few times until after World War II. Regardless of when or where we met, he was always so gracious and made me think he was so glad to see me.

My discharge from the Army came October 16, 1945, and I opened my office for practice of general surgery and obstetrics in Clinton, Kentucky, November 27, 1945. Soon after that date, I developed three primary interests, (1) my practice, (2) keeping my family healthy, and (3) Kentucky basketball. Needless to say, that last interest soon led to the lasting, close friendship with Coach Rupp.

Coach Adolph F. Rupp
Memorial Coliseum
Lexington, Kentucky

Chocolate Refrigerator Cake

1 7-ounce package semi-sweet chocolate pieces
1 square bitter chocolate
2 tablespoons sugar
3 tablespoons cold water
3 eggs, separated
1 cup heavy cream, whipped
1 teaspoon vanilla
1/4 teaspoon peppermint flavoring
18 ladyfingers, split

Melt chocolate in double boiler. Add sugar and water; mix well. Remove from heat. Gradually stir into egg yolks and beat smooth with spoon; cool. Beat egg whites stiff and fold into chocolate mixture. Fold in whipped cream and flavorings. Arrange some of the ladyfingers on the bottom of a loaf pan and pour in some of the chocolate and whipped cream mixture. Then alternate layers of ladyfingers and chocolate mixture until all has been used having ladyfingers on top. Chill in refrigerator for 24 hours. Turn out onto platter, slice and serve with whipped cream and nuts.
Serves 12.

Adolph F. Rupp

Chapter II

In late February, 1946, I took advantage of the excellent train service to Louisville and went to see the SEC tournament. Since that was such a fantastic tournament from our point of view, and also my first post World War II tournament, I want to show the results and also mention two players who later became my friends as well as outstanding basketball players and All-Americans. The team's season record was won 28, lost 2.

SEC tournament record, 1946:

February 28,	UK 69, Auburn 24
March 1,	UK 69, Florida 32
March 2, afternoon	UK 59, Alabama 30
March 2, evening	UK 59, LSU 36 (Final)

Ralph Beard and Wallace Jones were both freshman and starters. Beard was All-American the next 3 years, 1947, '48, and '49. Jones was All-American 1949. Both were later members of the famous Fabulous Five.

This was the actual beginning of my following the UK basketball team whenever possible. Because this represents the era of what many people consider the University of Kentucky's greatest basketball period, I would feel remiss not to mention some of the other great teams of that period.

As the record will show, the 1946 - 47 team was another great one, winning 34 and losing only 3. The team included Alex Groza, Cliff Barker and Kenneth Rollins (who became starters on the Fabulous Five the following year) and Joe Holland.

SEC tournament record 1947:

February 27,	UK 98, Vanderbilt 29
February 28,	UK 84, Auburn 18
March 1, afternoon	UK 75, Georgia Tech 53
March 1, evening	UK 55, Tulane 38 (Final)

I well remember this tournament. I actually felt sorry for the other teams. Each one looked whipped while warming up for the Kentucky slaughter.

Then came the famous Fabulous Five in 1947 - 48. Many people think this was the greatest collegiate basketball team of all time. Four starters were All-Americans with two such players on the bench. Cliff Barker was the best ball handler I have ever seen. He learned the art by constantly playing with a volley ball while a prisoner of war in Germany during World War II. When he thought Adolph was not looking, his antics often confused his team mates. He was actually a magician with a ball and it was almost impossible for an opponent to steal the basketball from him. It was a real show to watch him tease an opponent who was trying to steal the ball from him. I never saw one succeed.

I shall never forget the "slight-of-hand" trick Cliff pulled on DePaul in Louisville the night of December 10, 1947. I had an end seat on the front row almost under the basket that night and was sitting only a few feet from Cliff when he pulled the stunt. UK had the ball out of bounds under DePaul's basket and

Cliff was going to put the ball in play. When he was ready to pass the ball in bound, he signaled the others to break for the basket. As they did so, the entire DePaul team broke with them. Cliff apparently made an overhead pass, but instead of releasing the ball as the DePaul players thought he had, he held the ball and hid it behind his back. The crowd really roared and the opponents were actually bewildered. They did not know where the ball was, and Adolph was beside himself. He thought sure the officials would award the ball to DePaul, but Cliff took care of that too and got the ball to Ralph Beard in plenty of time.

I just have to mention one more member of this Fabulous Five team who was from my end of the state, from Wickliffe, Kentucky. Kenny Rollins was the captain of this great team and a real defensive whiz. What makes this little story so interesting is the fact that Kenny came close to selecting a college other than UK. Kenny is quoted as saying, "In my wildest dreams I never dreamed of coming to Kentucky. I went to Bowling Green and tried out for five or six days for Uncle Ed Diddle. He finally told me, 'Kenny, you have the talent, but you are a little small for my style of basketball, and I don't have any more scholarships available for small men.' I was crushed. So were Mom and Dad. We had just about given up any thought of me getting a scholarship in basketball when I got a letter from Rupp inviting me to UK."

"Adolph had called in 35 boys from all over the USA. He sat on one side of the floor, and Paul McBrayer sat on the other side. After five or six days of intensive scrimmages and workouts, I was one of those he selected. I doubt that I've sensed any greater feeling than when he told me I was one of the five. Perhaps winning the gold medal in the 1948 Olympics equated it." (From *Kentucky Basketball* by Russell Rice, p. 137).

SEC tournament 1948 in Louisville:

March 4,	UK 87, Florida 31
March 5,	UK 63, LSU 47
March 6, afternoon	UK 70, Tennessee 49

March 6, evening   UK 54, Georgia Tech 43 (Final)

NCAA tournament in New York City:

March 18,   UK 76, Columbia 53
March 20,   UK 60, Holy Cross 52
March 23,   UK 58, Baylor 42 (Final)

After winning the National Championship, this team combined with the Phillips Oilers to form the Olympic team to represent the USA. They went to London and won the World Championship during the summer of 1948.

By this time I had become a pretty regular fan at our "away" games and usually served as what some people called "the traveling team physician." I also took care of Adolph's minor ailments on these trips. At that time the University had never had a basketball team physician who traveled with the team. I was a railroad surgeon during those years and had an annual pass which made it quite "convenient" to attend games in Memphis, New Orleans, St. Louis, Chicago, Auburn, and Louisville. It was still almost impossible to get tickets in Alumni Gym, so I never tried. Nashville, Oxford and Starkville, Mississippi were within easy driving distance and they usually had tickets for sale. But if not, Adolph took care of me.

The 1948 - 49 team was another power house with a fabulous season. It won 32, lost 2. It also won the SEC tournament and the NCAA by lopsided scores. Coach Rupp was so proud of this team, which was largely the same as the 1947 - 48 team, and he wanted people in other parts of Kentucky and Tennessee to see them play. So he arranged to have the Ole Miss game played in Memphis on February 5, 1949.

The coach got us tickets and I took a carload of family members to the game.

This one incident is an example of how even people in Memphis felt about Kentucky's basketball. I parked my car at the hotel front entrance while we ate. When time came to go to the game, which was within walking distance, the hotel manager told me to just leave my car where it was, assuring me that the police would not bother the car if we were there for that Kentucky game. A lot of people from extreme Western Kentucky saw that game and it was a favorite conversation subject for a long time afterwards. The final score was UK 75, Ole Miss 45.

Several years later in 1955 a big celebration was held for Coach Rupp commemorating his twenty-fifth anniversary as Head Basketball Coach at University of Kentucky. Among other gifts, he was presented a new Cadillac.

Several people made short talks and told some interesting stories about the coach, one of which was told by the well known student manager, Humpsey Yessin. Humpsey said they were playing Arkansas State one night and the score was 35 to 3 at the end of the first half. When they went to the dressing room, Coach looked at the score book and saw that number 12 had made the three points, one basket and one free throw. He looked at the team and asked, "Who is guarding that #12?"

Beard spoke up and said, "He is my man, coach."

"Well get on him, Ralph. He's running wild out there."

I think mention should be made here of UK's first seven-foot player, Bill Spivey. It has been said that Bill's nickname was Grits because he ate so much grits as a child in Georgia. It was also said that Georgia and Georgia Tech both declined to give him a scholarship because he was so "skinny" and awkward. As one might expect, when a 7-foot, 160 pound kid came to UK to play basketball many stories were told about him, one of which I like because it sounded so much like Adolph; Coach Lancaster supposedly called Adolph to say a 7-foot beanpole of a kid was in the office and wanted to play basketball for UK. Adolph told Harry to sign him before he changed his mind but Harry said, "Coach, I watched this kid work out and he is hopeless."

"You say he is seven feet tall?"

"Yes, and weighs only 160 pounds."

"Sign the son-of-a-bitch, Harry. He'll play or we'll kill him."

Well, Bill got his scholarship contract and agreed to spend the summer in Lexington where he worked in a drug store. As the story goes, he got the drugstore job because he could change the light bulbs in the ceiling lights without using a ladder. The druggist was told to let Bill have all the food, including milk shakes, malted milks and ice cream he wanted. Each time Bill gained a few pounds, Harry would cable Adolph in London and tell him how much Bill had gained. After a number of messages, Adolph called Harry and said, "Harry, you have convinced me the Spivey kid can eat, but can he play basketball?"

Bill developed into an All-American his junior year, and really convinced his critics that he was the nation's #1 center in the game with Kansas in Memorial Auditorium December 16, 1950. Quite awhile before that game, sports writers agreed the game would decide whether Kansas or Kentucky had the #1 center.

About midway through the second half, Kansas' big center fouled out when the game was practically won by a big score. Since the Kansas coach was Adolph's former coach at Kansas, he did a most unique and gentlemanly thing by taking Bill out of the game so as not to be unfair to his former coach. Bill had completely dominated the game. UK went on to win 68 to 39. Just two days before, UK had defeated Florida 85 to 37. That team also won 32 and lost 2, including the NCAA National Championship, March 3, 1951.

I remember well our game with Bradley University on February 5, 1949, in Owensboro. A lawyer in Clinton who for some unknown reason was always against the University of Kentucky, sat behind our bench. He continually harassed Coach Rupp until finally, during the second half after he had positioned himself immediately behind the coach, Adolph turned and said, "Mister why in the heck don't you go there?"

That same year, after we were scheduled to play Oklahoma A & M in the final NCAA game in Seattle, Washington on March 26, 1949, that same lawyer stopped me after a Rotary Club meeting and wanted to bet $10 on A & M. I said, "No, I won't make such a bet as that because I don't want to lose your friendship for a lousy ten dollars, but if you are sincere about wanting to bet on Oklahoma A & M, I'll bet you $500 or more and put the money in the Clinton Bank." He lost all interest in betting against Kentucky, and our mild friendship was saved. Incidentally, we won the game 46 to 36. Since it was my birthday, he should have known those players would not let me down.

Kentucky's winning ways continued and we won the next SEC tournament in Louisville March 4, 1950, by defeating Tennessee 95 to 58. That was such a sweet victory. The band marched several blocks before entering the Kentucky hotel for a post game rendition. A large crowd of happy fans marched behind the band, including some members of my family.

I shall never forget Coach Rupp standing on the steps in the hotel lobby while the band played "On, On U of K." He was so pleased that he joined in the celebration and, as usual, thanked everyone for their support.

But a year later, the worm turned. In the final game of the SEC tournament March 3, 1951, which we were favored to win by another big score, Vanderbilt upset Kentucky 61 to 57. Boy howdy. Whatta blow.

After the game, Adolph asked me to go to Spivey's hotel room and examine him. He had not played well and the coach thought he might be sick. As it turned out, Bill had a very mild throat infection but he did not use that as an alibi for the defeat.

This 1950 - 51 team was the first to play in the new Memorial Coliseum. UK defeated Purdue University 70 to 52 December 9, 1950 in the dedication game. After losing that game to Vanderbilt, this team finished with quite a record, 32 wins and 2 losses. They also won the NCAA championship again by defeating Kansas State 68 to 58 in the final game March 27, 1951 in Minneapolis, Minn.

The following year, Marie and I were in Lexington and wanted to see the new Coliseum. Coach Harry Lancaster very graciously showed us through the entire building. He was so proud of the place - even pointing out the fact that the ceiling was 49 feet above the floor. By this time Harry was also our friend, and his wife Louise, soon became one.

Well, a great thing happened the following year: Marie and I were married in the First Baptist Church of Clinton, Ky. December 27, 1951.

Kentucky was scheduled to play in the Sugar Bowl in New Orleans, December 28 and 29. I called Adolph three days before the wedding and asked him for two tickets to the Sugar Bowl. He said, "Doc, there is no way. The University only got 300 tickets and they are all gone."

I said, "Well I am really sorry - I'm getting married the twenty-seventh and wanted my bride to see those games."

"You are getting married?" Coach asked. "Hell, I'll send you two tickets today." And he did. After that he and Marie developed a close and lasting friendship. Needless to say, Esther, Adolph's wonderful wife, soon came into the fold and that friendship became so great that it later enveloped our respective families. Two finer friends, we have never had.

After the Coliseum opened, we started attending a lot of home games. We still did not have season tickets but that presented no problems. Coach Rupp always had tickets for us.

Soon after our marriage, the Lexington fans started inviting us to the "post game" parties, which we thoroughly enjoyed. Those parties also afforded us the opportunities to meet new friends - in Louisville as well as in Lexington. The Rupp's were always invited and he was really the life of the party. Needless to say, each game was discussed, "hashed and rehashed" a number of times. On rare occasions, some "know-it-all" who had imbibed too much would make a complete ass of himself by trying to tell the coach where he made some coaching mistakes during the game. That person was always absent from the next party. To say that those parties were attended by a "close-knit" crowd would really be a gross understatement.

Marie still says that if it had not been for Kentucky's basketball, she is not sure we would have had a wedding trip. We went to Dallas after the Sugar Bowl basketball and saw the football Wildcats win the Cotton Bowl.

The 1951 - 52 team was another fine one. It won 29, and lost 3. The team also won the SEC Tournament again by another set of big scores but got beat in the NCAA Eastern Regionals by St. Johns, 64 to 57 on March 22, 1952. We had defeated St. Johns on December 17, 81 to 40.

Bobby Watson, a 5' 10" guard from Owensboro, was the team captain. For the previous couple of years, the media had referred to Bobby as the runt, the roach, the midget, etc., and my 82 year old mother had never seen Bobby but thought of him as being no taller than 5' 3" or 4" at the most. He was her all-time favorite.

Adolph paid us a visit soon after the season and during lunch at our house, he got into a friendly argument with Mama about Bobby. Boy howdy, he really got a kick out of the reprimands she gave him for "mistreating" Bobby. Before leaving, however, he "confessed" to her that Bobby was one of his all-time favorites. A few days later, she received an autographed photo from Bobby that she cherished the remainder of her life.

Sometime later, Coach Rupp paid us another visit when he stopped by the hospital. As he arrived, I was removing a gallbladder and the young administrator came to the operating room door and said, "Doctor, a man is in the office and says he is Coach Rupp but I am sure he is an imposter. What do you want me to tell him?" It seems Howard had heard so much about the great coach he just could not believe he was actually there.

During 1952 - 53, there was no schedule because UK was under suspension by the NCAA due to infractions that happened in 1948 or 49, when our present players were in high school. The players agreed to practice all year and play some intra-squad game-type scrimmages.

Soon after the suspension became known, I was in Adolph's office and we were talking about it. He said "Doc, the so-called officials finally learned they cannot beat us on the basketball floor, so they suspended us for a season. Since we had won nine consecutive SEC Championships, they were determined we would not make it 10 in a row."

During that year of no schedule, Adolph developed what was called the "cyclone" offense. And the next year, the team frequently struck opponents like a cyclone. Cliff Hagan and Frank Ramsey were co-captains both years.

The season of 1953 - 54, UK won 25 and lost 0. This team just absolutely refused to get beat by anybody. I shall never forget the UKIT tournament that year. It was the first UKIT tournament and it was a honey. More about that later.

Long before practice started in the fall of 1953, this team had already garnered far more publicity than many teams get during an entire season. Expectations were unusually high and fans in Lexington were saying this may be Coach Rupp's best team ever. The results of the December games were certainly indicative of the team's readiness when the season opened.

December 5,	UK 86, Temple 59	Home
December 12,	UK 81, Xavier 66	Away
December 14,	UK 101, Wake Forest 69	Away
December 18,	UK 71, St. Louis 59	Away

The first UKIT:

December 21,	UK 85, Duke 69
December 22,	UK 73, LaSalle 60
	(championship game)

Marie and I went to St. Louis for the game there and that victory was almost as "sweet" as winning the first UKIT. St. Louis was favored by most sports writers, but those sports writers had not seen a UK team play for more than a year. Our fans could have told them differently.

Cliff Hagan, Frank Ramsey and Lou Tsioropoulos were our big scoring guns as well as the rebounders. They actually positioned themselves around the goal in such a manner that they formed an arc which made it extremely difficult for opponents to get rebounds.

It became apparent early in the second half that St. Louis could not rebound with this team - hence the outcome was pretty well settled by that time. Their star forward was completely dominated by Tsioropoulos in both offense and defense. In fact, he picked up three early fouls while trying to guard Lou. After that, "Church was out" and it was time to "put the chairs in the wagon and go home."

We enjoyed the St. Louis game so much that I called Coach Rupp after we got home and asked how to get two tickets for the UKIT. He told me he would leave them at the "will call" window.

Spinach Dip

1 box frozen chopped spinach
1/2 cup green onion, chopped
3/4 teaspoon salt
3/4 teaspoon pepper
2 cups mayonnaise

Thaw spinach and squeeze out all water. Mix all ingredients together. Chill overnight for full flavor. Serve with fresh vegetables for dipping.

Ralph Beard

Sausage-Bean Chowder

1 pound bulk pork sausage
1 16-ounce can kidney beans
1-1/2 cups canned tomatoes
2 cups water
1 small onion, chopped
1/2 cup potatoes, diced
1/4 cup green peppers, chopped
1 bay leaf
3/4 teaspoon salt
1/4 teaspoon garlic salt
1/4 teaspoon thyme
1/8 teaspoon black pepper

Cook sausage in skillet until lightly browned; drain off fat. In a large sauce pan, combine all ingredients. Simmer, covered, for 1 hour and 15 minutes. Remove bay leaf. Serves 4 to 6.

Note: This is the original recipe but I use a very large soup or canning pan and triple the recipe. I use 1 can each of kidney, pinto and navy beans. After cooking I freeze in containers for 2 and 4 servings. Great to have on hand for unexpected guests!

Kenny Rollins

Double Chocolate Cheesecake

Cheesecake filling:

8 1-ounce squares semi-sweet chocolate
3 8-ounce packages cream cheese, softened
1 cup sugar
2 eggs
2 teaspoons cocoa
1 teaspoon vanilla flavoring
1-1/2 cups commercial sour cream

Melt chocolate in top of double boiler. In a large mixer bowl cream softened cheese; add sugar gradually. Add eggs, one at a time, beating well after each addition. Add melted chocolate, cocoa, vanilla and sour cream; blend thoroughly. Pour over crumb crust. Bake at 350° for 45 minutes. Cake will still be soft, but will get firm as it chills. Allow to remain in pan; cool at room temperature for 1 hour. Refrigerate 5 to 6 hours before serving. Very, very rich. Serves 16.

Joe Holland

Southern Spoon Bread

1 cup white corn meal, sifted
2-1/2 cups milk, scalded
1 teaspoon salt
2 tablespoons butter or margarine, melted
4 eggs, separated
1 teaspoon baking powder
1 tablespoon sugar

Gradually add corn meal to scalded milk stirring until smooth; add salt and cook over hot water until thickened. Cool slightly; add beaten egg yolks, baking powder, sugar and butter. Fold in beaten egg whites. Place mixture in a well greased casserole and bake at 375° for 35 to 40 minutes.

Paul McBrayer

Chicken Caliente

3 pounds chicken, cooked, boned and cut up
1 large onion, chopped
1 large green pepper, chopped
2 tablespoons margarine
1 teaspoon chili powder
Garlic salt
1 10-3/4 ounce can mushroom soup
1 10-3/4 ounce can chicken soup
1 cup broth
1 10 ounce can Ro-Tel tomatoes
12 corn tortillas, cut in strips
8 ounces cheddar cheese

Sauté onion and pepper in margarine. Combine chili powder, garlic salt, chicken soup, mushroom soup, broth and Rotel. Layer 1/2 each of the chicken, soup mixture, tortilla strips, onion and pepper mixture, then cheese. Repeat layers. Cook covered at 350° for 30 minutes; uncover and bake 15 minutes longer.

Cliff Hagan

Pea Salad

2 15-ounce cans of peas, drained
3 eggs, hardboiled and chopped
1/2 small onion, minced
1/2 cup mayonnaise

Mix all ingredients together in a bowl. Cover and place in refrigerator overnight. Serve on lettuce leaf.

Frank Ramsey

Stuffed Grape Leaves (Dolmathes)

1-1/2 to 2 pounds lean ground beef
2 eggs
2 medium onions, chopped
1 cup uncooked instant rice
1/2 cup parsley, chopped
1 teaspoon fresh mint, chopped, optional
3 tablespoons olive oil
Water
Salt and pepper to taste
1 jar grape leaves
2 cups beef broth
Egg-Lemon Sauce

Mix beef and eggs. Add onion, rice, parsley, mint, olive oil and 1/4 cup water. Season with salt and pepper. Rinse leaves thoroughly to remove brine. Lay leaf, shiny side down, on counter and place a spoonful of meat mixture in center. Roll end once, then sides inward and continue to roll. Place folded side down in heavy, greased sauce pan. Place tightly side-by-side making more than one layer if needed. Invert plate to hold down. Add beef broth and 1-1/2 cups water. Cover and simmer 45 minutes. Serve with Egg-Lemon Sauce poured over top of each individual serving.

Egg-Lemon Sauce

1 can cream of chicken soup, undiluted
Lemon juice to taste

Stir and heat until warmed thoroughly.

Dolmathes may be refrigerated but make fresh sauce each time you reheat.

Recipe may be cut in half.

Lou Tsioropoulos

Chapter III

After the St. Louis game, Marie thought she should forego the UKIT and stay home with Donna and the family. So, "Pond," my brother, went with me instead.

In our first UKIT game the team easily disposed of Duke 85 to 69, confirming the fans earlier predictions of a great team. Our championship game the next night, however, did not start out that way. LaSalle broke out early and almost immediately to a 12 to 0 lead. I shall never forget Pond's reaction. He said, "Hell, Vester, we are going to get beat." I tried to reassure him and suggested Adolph would soon call a time out and make a few changes. And he did.

After that first time out with the score still 12 to 0, we scored the next 13 points and took the lead 13 to 12.

LaSalle's great All-American forward, Tom Gallo, was nothing less than awesome. For awhile early in the first half, he looked to be unstoppable. However, we had some pretty good country players too - plus the fact that sitting on our bench was the best coaching team the world had ever seen - Coach Adolph Rupp and his very excellent assistant, Coach Harry Lancaster.

The final score was UK 73, LaSalle 60.

I am not sure during which games the following episodes happened, but these little incidents indicate the respect the officials had for Coach Rupp and his players.

Butch Lampert, one of the fine SEC referees, told this to the Wildcat Club a short time after Adolph retired. It seems that Frank Ramsey was "walking" the basketball down the court and as he passed by Butch, he said, "Good game, Ref." When Butch agreed, Frank said, "Why in the hell don't you watch it then?"

Another time as Butch sauntered past our bench, Adolph called out to him, "Butch, who is that other son-of-a-bitch working with you?" Butch said he got half way down the court before the implication hit him. No technical foul was called either time.

Another time during this same season, Coach Rupp was displeased with Lou's play during the first half and apparently thought he should do more rebounding and less shooting and so expressed his feeling by saying, "Damn you Lou, get your ass on the boards and let somebody else shoot the damn thing." Even with this great team, anything less than perfect was not good enough.

During Hagan's first semester at UK, Coach Rupp usually encouraged the upper classmen to help the freshmen players to adapt to our offense more quickly. Well, Cliff still had one of his high school habits that was very irksome to both coaches. When the fast break offense would start, Cliff would break for the other end of the court and never look to see where the ball was. Bill Spivey was also fed up with this freshman who ignored the coaches' instructions and decided to teach him the hard way. So sure enough, when the fast break started this particular time, Cliff took-off like a jet and never looked back. Spivey grabbed the basketball and threw it as hard as he could, hitting Cliff in the back of his head and knocking him flat on his face. It is very doubtful that Cliff ever made that mistake again.

After that first UKIT on December 21 and 22, 1953, the team proceeded to more or less make a mockery of the Southeastern Conference by winning every game by lopsided scores. However, due to a schedule disagreement, LSU officials claimed they had not officially lost a conference game (UK did not play a regular season game against LSU that year) and they demanded a playoff game on a neutral floor. So it was arranged for the two teams to meet in a playoff game in Vanderbilt's gym March 9, 1954.

Coach Rupp arranged for our front row seats and Marie and I attended a truly great game. In fact, I served as team physician again that night.

Vanderbilt's gym was fairly new with a seating capacity of only 8000. A Vandy couple was seated next to us and I asked the gentleman why they built such a small gym. He said, "The only time we ever fill this place is when Kentucky plays here."

There was a distinct feeling of grudge between these two teams and this game rapidly developed into one of fierce competition. LSU had a real fine 6' 9" center, Bob Pettit. Early in the game, it became apparent that they had a game plan that was not exactly illegal or against the rules, but it was extremely unusual, to say the least.

When any other LSU player was shooting a free throw, Pettit was always lined up next to the goal with the backboard to his right. The last free throw invariably struck the basket just hard enough to gently bounce back barely above the rim and Petit would very cunningly tap the ball back so it would fall through the hoop for two points instead of one. That little "off-color" trick not only kept LSU in the game, but it almost beat us and might have except for our great coaching.

Late in the game with LSU leading by 3 points and less than four minutes to play, Gale Rose more or less took charge. We scored and as they started up the floor, Gale stole the ball just as the dribbler crossed the free throw line, made a perfect pass to Frank Ramsey who went in for an easy lay-up. They pulled the same trick three more times and we went on to win 63 to 56.

The irony of that stupid ruling that made those players ineligible was later referred to by a highly intelligent sports columnist for the *Louisville Courier-Journal*. He knew that if the three had failed one course and had not received their degrees, they would have been eligible, so he wrote: "It was, and is, a proud group of men, the 1953 - 54 University of Kentucky basketball team that finished the season undefeated and ranked Number 1 in the nation - and then said no to an NCAA bid because three of its players were too smart. (From *The Courier Journal* 10/16/86)

Immediately after the news broke, I looked at Adolph and realized he was sick. A quick examination revealed his heart to be markedly irregular. We took him directly to his hotel room and put him to bed. I gave him a pretty strong injection to relieve his chest pain and also to relax him so he could rest.

After the coach quieted down a bit, Marie and I started to leave for Clinton, a distance of about 160 miles. But Rupp awoke and said, "Doc, don't leave me yet." We stayed with him until 2:00 in the morning when he told us he felt much better and for us to go on home, unless we could stay all night. Fortunately, he was able to return to Lexington the next day and was out and about in a few days.

1/22/79, Kentucky dressing room in Rupp arena. Left to right, Truman Claytor, Torry Sosby (1/2 face), Chuck Verderber, Kyle Macy, Dr. V. A. Jackson

Coach Rupp, Dr. V. A. Jackson visiting friend, Hugh Lattus, in Hickman, KY

Coach Rupp, the team, Dr. Jackson and spectators at a game in Dayton, Ohio.
Photo courtesy of Dave Lutes, Dayton, Ohio.

Dr. Jackson, Coach Rupp,
Doris Lattus

Dr. Jackson and Coach Rupp exiting private plane to attend a
dinner in Hickman, KY   9/25/70

Coach Rupp
and Dr. Jackson

Coach Rupp, Dr. Jackson and trainer, Bobby Barton

Dr. Jackson, Marie Jackson, and friend Carol Smith owner of Cornerstone Bookstore, Lexington, at a cookbook signing, 7/19/86

Dr. Jackson Secretariat at Claiborne Farm in Paris, KY

Coach Rupp, Hugh Lattus and Dr. Jackson

*Coach Rupp, Dr. Jackson and Larry Stamper (far right) at The Sorghum Festival ,
West Liberty, KY, October, 1974*

Chapter IV

A month or so later, after the NCAA tournament, Adolph paid us another visit. By this time, I was on the committee to help start the UK Medical School. The coach was on his way to Hickman, Kentucky, to speak at a high school banquet. He was aware of the fact that Judge Elvis Starr Sr. was also scheduled to speak about the medical school at the same banquet and he wanted Marie and me to go with him and we did.

Judge Starr was the Circuit Judge. He was also the father of Elvis Starr Jr. who came close to becoming the President of the University of Kentucky and later became President of Indiana University, as well as Secretary of the Army. Both men were good friends of mine.

Adolph was introduced as the banquet's first speaker and, as always, set everybody at ease with his opening remarks. He looked the crowd over and said, "My, what a wonderful dinner. Your people really know how to prepare and serve good food. This is the very first banquet I have attended this year where they didn't serve green peas. I have eaten so many green peas the last few weeks, the damn things are almost running out of my ears."

Needless to say, he kept the crowd spellbound for the entire 40 minutes. He was a fantastic after-dinner speaker - and he never used notes. But, more about that later.

Judge Starr was the next speaker and when he was introduced, the other two doctors present got up and walked out. They knew the judge was going to speak in favor of the state building a medical school in Lexington and they were strongly opposed to it.

The "walkout" caused some embarrassment, but the judge did not let it deter him, and he too gave a very interesting and informative talk. That fierce opposition from my colleagues who opposed the new medical school resulted in my being criticized for serving on the committee.

Coach Rupp visited us in 1954 before the start of basketball practice when we moved into our new home. After we had shown him through the place, the three of us were in the kitchen when he looked around and said, "God, this is so beautiful. I sure don't want Esther to see it." That was his way of letting us know he really liked the place.

I remember visiting Adolph and Harry in the office at the Coliseum during the summer of 1954. Harry very casually told me that a professor had turned in his two priorities for season tickets. He then said, "Doc, I wish you would tell the ticket manager you want those tickets because the time may come when tickets will get scarce. You won't need season tickets, of course, as long as Adolph and I are here but one never knows what may happen." Needless to say, I agreed and the two of us went directly to the ticket office. That was the beginning of my season ticket priority. It's really surprising the number of people who have asked me "How in the hell did you get season tickets when you lived in Clinton?" I wanted to tell each one, "It was easy." But I never did.

Later that summer, we had a visiting high school team play in Clinton that had one outstanding player who I realized would be a fine college prospect. His coach told me after the game that the kid just "came-into-his-own" the latter part of the first semester. He also said the kid was an A-student and planned to study chemistry in college. So I hot-footed it to Lexington the next day, covering 330 miles of 2 lane roads, to tell Adolph about him.

When I told Adolph of the kid's qualifications, how he would fit right into our style of play, etc., he exploded. He said, "Doc, why in the hell didn't you tell me about this kid earlier? We have used up our last scholarship and now there is no way we can take him."

I told him that I had seen him play less than 20 hours ago for the first time myself and had not actually heard of him before then. Well, the boy graduated from high school with honors, went to Vanderbilt on a basketball scholarship and made a star player there. He later told me he was happy at "Vandy," which was a great school, but when he was in high school, his first choice was Kentucky.

Although our undefeated team of 1953 - 54 was all but destroyed by graduation, Coach Rupp, as usual, came back with another fine team the following year, 1954 - 55, and won 23 games while only losing 3.

Bob Burrow, a 6' 7" junior college graduate from Texas was our center. He was a good one and made All-American the following year, 1955 - 56.

Since we had season tickets, we missed very few games this year and Donna, our 8 year old daughter, usually went with us. Bill Hunt's Sporting Goods store in Mayfield, Kentucky, was the supplier for UK's uniforms at this time. He saw Donna a few times and then had a UK cheerleader's sweater made for her. Our seats were on the fourth row in the center section and the first night she wore that sweater, the cheerleaders asked her to be their mascot for the game. She was a regular performer after that and developed a "puppy love" for Bob Burrow. She thought he was the "prettiest" player on the team.

We won the UKIT by defeating LaSalle again, 63 to 54.

On December 30, 1954, we defeated St. Louis 82 to 65 for our 129th consecutive home game win. But in our next home game that was against a supposedly weak team, January 8, 1955, Georgia Tech broke that string of home victories by defeating Kentucky 59 to 58. UNBELIEVABLE.

We missed that horrid upset game because I had pinned a broken hip for a man that morning and could not leave him overnight so soon. I never made such a mistake in scheduling major operations again. We were there January 10, 1955, two days after the Georgia Tech debacle, for our game with DePaul, a team that was rated much higher than Georgia Tech.

Boy howdy. That DePaul game was something to behold. It was really a close game the first half and a lot of fans were thinking about two nights ago. As Adolph was to tell the press later, however, he "took them to the woodshed" between the halves. Surprisingly, the paint did not actually crumble off the dressing room walls during that intermission, but the players got the message. During the first ten minutes of the second half, UK outscored DePaul 43 to 10. The final score was 92 to 59. Talk about great coaching. That was a masterpiece.

Coach Ray Meyer of DePaul was such a fine gentleman and also a very close friend of Coach Rupp. I'm not at all sure Adolph really wanted to beat him so decisively. Oh, Coach Rupp wanted to win alright, but I doubt that he wanted to embarrass his longtime friend.

After the game, Coach Meyer went to Adolph and congratulated him, then said, "Adolph, I am sorry we came in here and stunk up this nice place this way. You get the building fumigated tomorrow and send me the bill."

One time we were playing DePaul in Chicago and I needed two extra tickets so I wrote Coach Meyer. He wrote me by return mail and said he would have two tickets for me any time I wanted them. He added, "Any man who is a friend of Adolph is a friend of mine." I never forgot that.

Miss Helen King and her sister, Miss Willie, must have been blessed with a real intuitive message concerning that DePaul game, because they sent out invitations before the game for a party they were having in their home after the game. And that was no ordinary party. I am sure I have never been to a more appropriate or to a more enjoyable party any place or any time than theirs.

We were scheduled to play Tulane and LSU the following weekend. Back then, before TV, most of our games were played on Saturday and Monday nights.

When somebody mentioned the upcoming game with Tulane the following Saturday, Harry turned to me and asked, "Doc, why don't you and Marie go to that game?" I told him we would certainly like to so he then suggested we go into the other room and put the bee in Adolph for two tickets, which we did.

Adolph's first question was, "What about the LSU game Monday? Since you will already be down there you might as well see both games." I explained to him that we would be traveling by train and that train did not go through Baton Rouge. "Why hell, that's no problem. We have some extra seats in the plane and after the game, we can fly you two to another town where the damn train will stop and pick you up," he countered. I explained that such an arrangement would cause me to miss office practice both Monday and Tuesday. Then he let me have it. "Well, by God, Doc, if you are so damn poor you cannot afford to miss two days from practice to see this team play LSU, you had better miss both games. Hell no. I won't get you tickets for either game." That blustery comeback of his did not upset me at all because I knew that was his way of telling me he would have tickets for us but he was disappointed because we would not be able to continue on to LSU. Marie was not too sure of getting the tickets, but she later learned more about the coach and his unorthodox ways of saying things and how to interpret him. Needless to say, we thoroughly enjoyed that Tulane game which we won 58 to 44. Also we were back in the office Monday morning and listened to UK defeat LSU 64 to 62 that night.

One more reference concerning this very surprising season. On January 31, 1955, in Atlanta, Georgia Tech again upset UK, this time 65 to 59. Those were our only SEC losses and, I think, Georgia Tech's only SEC wins that year. However we easily won the SEC Championship and played in the NCAA tournament March 11 and 12, 1955 in Evanston, Illinois.

We lost our first game to Marquette 79 to 71 and then won the consolation game by defeating Penn State 84 to 59.

During our game with Marquette, Bob Burrow was at the line for a free throw and as he bounced the basketball, the crowd became unusually quiet and, just as Bob started to shoot the free throw, our daughter Donna called out in her childhood voice, "Make it, Bobby." Bob turned and looked in her direction and the crowd really laughed. Adolph enjoyed her encouraging remark, too.

As we all proceeded into the hotel lobby after the game, Adolph picked up Donna and gave her a big hug. He sensed her embarrassment and quickly told her, "I have been hugging Herky like this for a long time and if I can keep hugging you, you will soon grow to be as big as Bob Burrow there." That really made her day.

Gale Rose, who had been one of my favorites for a long time, was voted the tournament's outstanding player. He was really terrific in both games.

Gale was a flashy guard from Paris, Kentucky, and he could really play basketball. During his senior year in high school, he was rated near the top nationally. He was a starting guard on the 1953 - 54 undefeated team. However, during the season, he was ridden pretty hard by the coach. Dan Chandler said that once in practice Adolph said "Dammit, Rose, you really do look like a Shetland pony in a stud horse parade."

Before Gale was a starter, Dan said, "Doc, he has the ability and determination to be a starter but he just will not rough it up and play in scrimmage as if he is willing to knock the teeth from his good friends. And, Adolph is not going to start anyone that does not go all out in practice even if it means roughing up his best friends. Gale is just too damn nice." But he had too much basketball ability to be denied a starting position. Gale went on to practice pharmacy in Eastern Kentucky.

In 1955 - 56, UK won 20, lost 6.

The win - loss record shows this was another fine season - at least most coaches would think so, but not Coach Rupp. UK not only let Temple beat them 73 to 61 at home, December 10, 1955 but Dayton did it in the final game of the UKIT December 21 after we had defeated a fine Minnesota team 72 to 65 the night before.

We drove to St. Louis on December 28, 1955 for our game with St. Louis. We won that game 101 to 80 so after the game a few of us got together in Claud Sullivan's room for a little celebration party. Claud called Adolph and asked him to come down. He sorta protested and said he was already dressed for bed and guessed he would miss the party. Claud said, "Oh hell, Adolph, you can sleep later. Doc and Marie are here and we want you to come."

"Doc and Marie are there?" Rupp asked. "Well tell 'em I'm not dressed but I'll be right down."

Adolph was wearing his bright scarlet red silk pajamas and when he entered the elevator, the attendant said, "Well, here comes Santa Claus without his beard."

Needless to say, after the coach arrived the place really came alive.

Time kept marching on that year. Vanderbilt beat us 81 to 73 in Nashville and Alabama stomped us 101 to 77 in Montgomery. Boy what a licking! Alabama won the SEC (there was no tournament then) but declined the bid to play in the NCAA so UK represented the SEC again, with these results:

March 16,   UK 84, Wayne U 64
March 17,   UK 77, Iona 89 in Iowa City

I attended most of our games, as usual, including the last two in Iowa City. The memories of that trip to Iowa City still linger. I flew with two of the tournament officials from Chicago in a DC-3 plane. After the tournament, I was unable to get plane passage home but a newsman heard of my plight and gave me a ride all the way home in his car. I was sure thankful Marie had decided not to make the trip.

After attending the annual meeting of the AMA in Chicago in June, 1956, Marie, Donna and I visited friends in Los Angeles. We three fell for the place and decided to move there. I went back to Los Angeles in August and took the examination for a California license and passed it. We moved in September, 1956.

In the meantime, about the middle of summer a real surprise happened. But let me quote Vernon Hatton from his book about Coach Rupp:

> *At times we felt that Coach Rupp didn't praise or respect us enough ,if you will, his players for the outstanding job they (we) were doing. We were never sure of anything, starting positions from year to year, making the traveling squad, or if we would get our tickets to the ball games or not. We really loved to hear Coach Rupp praise us and we often thought up ways to gain his respect.*

Vernon, one season, used this little system to keep Rupp off guard.

> *I had different people call Coach, and tell him I was going to drop out of school, and finish somewhere else. I never knew what results I was getting, except on one occasion. I was working at Kentucky Dam Village State Park, and at that time Bill Spivey was operating a golf driving range there. I asked Bill to help me and finally he gave in and called Coach Rupp, and told him that he had heard rumors that I was going to drop out and go to another school. Boy, did this get some action. The next morning, Dr. Jackson, from Western*

*Kentucky area, was on my doorsteps telling me
what a great mistake it would be to leave
Kentucky. I acted surprised, but still gave him
the impression he might be right. At the end
of summer I returned to Lexington, went to see
Coach Rupp and that was the first time I had
seen Coach Rupp so friendly.*
     (From From Both Ends of The Bench.)

It is only fair to our readers that they are made aware of a few facts about the above incidents.

Since I had been unusually busy during the summer, I didn't know anything about all of the schemes and so forth the players had been cooking up to enable them to sort of soften up the coach a little during the off season. As Vernon said in his book, I was totally unaware of what was going on until Coach Lancaster called.

Harry called the night before I went to see Vernon. It was obvious that he was definitely concerned about the developments and he let me know that Coach Rupp was equally concerned. He said they did not know which school "Vern" was leaning toward, but Murray State, Texas and a school in California were each putting the pressure on him to transfer to that particular school. Then he wanted to know if I would go see Vernon and try to "talk some sense into his head."

I tried to tell Harry that it was very doubtful I had enough influence with Vernon to be of any help. But he assured me that Vernon was very fond of me, and Harry and Adolph both thought that I could do more with him than anybody else. I finally agreed to go and he gave me the directions to Vernon's place on the lake.

Early the next morning, I went the 50 miles or so to the lake in order to catch Vernon in his cabin before he left for work. He was still there and seemed very much surprised and glad to see me.

He readily admitted he was seriously considering going elsewhere, but immediately said he was not going to Murray.

Then he gave me the "low-down."   He said, "Doc, as you know, that cash scholarship they give me is only $117.50 a month (He lived at home with his family) and I want to get married but that is not enough to live on."

"One school has offered me the same amount of money, plus a nice apartment, rent free with all utilities plus, a free car, plus $300 a month. Now, tell me, what would you do under these circumstances?"

"Vernon," I told him, "I know how you feel and, frankly, I don't blame you a damn bit and it would certainly be a big temptation for me. However, there is another factor that you may not have thought of."

"What's that?" He asked.

"We both know that your home is in Lexington, your people are there and they are quite anxious to watch you play. Also you are destined to be an All-American next year and all of your friends know you really want to stay in Lexington - and so do the people in the NCAA headquarters. Now, if you, the most publicized sophomore basketball player in the nation, suddenly leave your hometown and lifelong friends to attend another school, it will certainly raise a lot of eyebrows. Also, the NCAA will investigate you with a fine tooth comb. Frankly, if you do transfer, I am sincerely afraid they will declare you ineligible and end your college basketball career and perhaps ruin your chance of ever playing pro ball."

He looked down at the floor for a few seconds then said, "I want to talk to Coach Rupp before doing anything."

A few days later, Harry called me again and said, "Doc, I don't know what you said to Vernon, but whatever it was, it must have sunk in pretty deep because he is back with us to stay and seems perfectly happy. Thank you, my friend, for helping us out. We both appreciate what you did."

It was a few years later before I learned that Vernon's part was actually a hoax. As Paul Harvey would say, "Now we all know the rest of the story."

Let me just say, Vernon and I are still the best of friends.

That friendship has also included Marie for the last several years - twenty or more.

The following episode was told by Rev. Ed Beck who was the featured speaker at the annual 101 pre-season basketball banquet November 13, 1986. Harry Lancaster had told me the same story soon after the game mentioned in the story and it was so typical of Adolph's and Harry's dressing room remarks, I want to repeat it here for our readers to enjoy.

We were playing St. Louis and just after our players started warming up at our designated basket, the St. Louis players came out and sorta infiltrated into our group. Their big center grabbed the next rebound and threw it up into the stands. The crowd roared its approval. Of course, Beck walked over to him and said, "You should not have done that." But he did the same thing with the next rebound. This time Ed let him know that it was a sure way to get the hell knocked out of him. It created such a stir, Adolph immediately took the team to the dressing room.

Outside the dressing room, Adolph removed his coat as always, walked up to Ed and said, "You just embarrassed our team and our coaches. You big overgrown 6' 8" giant, you should be ashamed of yourself. Don't you have any guts? Do you know what that bunch of sonofabitches want? They want our basket the first half. Do you know what they want? Those overbearing bastards want our bench. Are you going to give in to them like a Mr. Milk Toast and let them have our bench that we know is ours?"

By this time, every player was as mad as a hornet. The usual placid and calm Vernon Hatton, with tears running down his cheeks, stood up and said, "Hell no, they are not going to get our bench or our basket. Let's go."

Adolph said, "Just a minute, fellows! Harry, do you think they are ready?"

"No, Coach, I don't think they are ready," Harry said.

Beck ran over to Harry, grabbed him by his shoulders, lifted him off the floor, shook him a few times and said, "What the hell do you mean? You know damn well we are ready."

He loosened his grip on Harry and Harry said, "Coach, I

think they are ready." Adolph said later they almost tore the door off its hinges getting out. We kept our bench and used the basket we were supposed to use and won 73 to 60.

The following little incident shows how much confidence Adolph had in Harry's ability and his knowledge of basketball. He sent Harry to scout Notre Dame in their last game before we were scheduled to play them. Unknown to Harry, Adolph also employed an outside scout to report on Notre Dame's game the same date.

Well, when Harry made his report to Adolph, it was at variance in almost every detail with the other man's report. So Adolph showed it to Harry and said "Hell, Harry, now I don't know what to do."

Harry said, "Adolph, I watched that game and wrote the report as I saw it - Now, you have paid your money so, you can have a choice."

Adolph's answer was, "Hell, I'm going with your report. If I wanted a damn rubber stamp I could buy one for 50 cents - a helluva lot less expensive than you are."

They sometimes disagreed, but they always later had a "meeting-of-the-minds" and they actually worked together like a hand in a glove.

Bob's Corn Meal Muffins

1-1/4 cups corn meal
1/2 cup flour
1 teaspoon salt
2 teaspoons baking powder
1 tablespoon sugar
1 egg, beaten, or 1/2 carton egg substitute
1/3 cup oil
1 cup milk

Combine all ingredients and put in greased or sprayed muffin tins that have been heated. Cook at 400° for about 20 minutes or until brown. Stand muffins on sides the last 2 to 3 minutes to get a crisp muffin bottom.

Bob Burrow

Broccoli Casserole

2 boxes frozen broccoli, cooked and drained
1/2 cup butter, divided
1/2 pound Velvetta cheese
18 Ritz crackers, crumbled

Place cooked broccoli into a casserole dish. Melt 1/4 cup butter and stir in cheese until melted; pour over broccoli. Melt remaining 1/4 cup butter and mix with crumbled crackers. Spread over top of broccoli mixture. Bake at 350° for 20 minutes.

Herky Rupp

Sweet Potato Soufflé

1 29-ounce can sweet potatoes, drained
1/2 cup butter, melted
1/2 cup sugar
1/8 teaspoon cloves
1 egg
1/4 teaspoon nutmeg
1/4 teaspoon mace
1 6-ounce can evaporated milk

Blend all ingredients with electric mixer; pour into buttered casserole dish. Bake 40-60 minutes at 375°.

Reverend Ed Beck

Chapter V

As stated earlier, we moved to Los Angeles in September, 1956, and set up practice there. To our surprise, my practice in Los Angeles developed in "leaps and bounds" - much faster than we dared to hope.

Fortunately, most of my early patients preferred to use the Culver City Hospital - one that was frequented by quite a few movie stars. Soon after I gained staff privileges for major surgery, the Hospital Administrator told me two very busy General Practitioners who did not practice surgery were in the market for a general surgeon. We three soon made an agreement. By that time, I was on the staff of two other nice hospitals and also had a pretty good office practice.

Donna was in school and the future looked bright indeed. About the first of December, however, we started getting letters from our former patients back home telling us the hospital was getting in financial trouble and unless we moved back it would probably have to close because they could not get a good surgeon to locate in such a small town.

Marie was already homesick and those letters greatly increased the severity of her illness. She went home for Christmas primarily to check the hospital conditions and confirmed the disturbing reports we had been getting. Finally, we started plans to move back to Clinton, which we did in January, 1957.

Fortunately, Harry Lancaster held my season tickets for us and refused to let anyone have them because, as he said later, he knew we would soon be back. I am sure glad he felt that way since tickets were not too easy to get by this time.

The Ole Miss game was played in Memphis a short time after we got settled again in Clinton, February 8, 1957, so we went.

This was just a short time after Vernon had his appendectomy and there was some doubt that we could win without him. Finally, it was decided that if he didn't chase any loose balls or mix it up too vigorously, it would be safe for him to play. Needless to say he tried to assure Adolph he was ready.

Even though Vernon was most certainly not up to par, his being in the game was a big boost to the team's morale and he definitely helped us win 75 to 69.

After the game, Fred Hurd came around and said, "Well, Doc, when the 'Old Pro' came in, it made a big difference." And it did.

In the dressing room after the game, Adolph called me to the side and told me he was almost sure we would play a doubleheader in Los Angeles in the fall of 1959 and he sure would like for us to be there. I promised we would.

Kentucky had another fine season, winning 23 and losing only 5. They also won the SEC but lost the second NCAA game March 16, 1957, 80 to 68 to Michigan State after defeating Pittsburgh 98 to 92, March 15, 1957.

The next year, 1957 - 58, our team was somewhat unpredictable, sorta up and down like a yo-yo. In fact, during the season when Adolph was holding a press conference and was asked about his players, his response was, "Well, gentlemen, let's face it. We have some pretty good players but if you had a bunch of musicians in an orchestra, you would probably have some violinists and perhaps some fiddlers. Well, on this basketball team we have several fiddlers but not real violinists. Perhaps an appropriate name for this crowd would be 'The Fiddling Five.'" That team which later won the National Championship is still affectionately known as the "The Fiddling Five." And I still love every one of them.

In spite of the team's somewhat erratic season, it still managed to win 23 and lose only 6, while playing a number of very fine teams.

A few games in particular during the regular season were really unusual in some respects.

Beating Temple 85 to 83 December 7, 1957, will always be a good conversation topic. With Temple leading by two points 71 to 69 and one second to play when UK called time out, it looked pretty hopeless. During the time out, Adolph asked Harry who he thought should take that easy last second shot. Harry said, "Let Vernon shoot it. He hasn't done anything else tonight so maybe he can hit one shot." That was Harry's way of prodding Vernon into doing a little more than he was capable of doing. He and Adolph both used that type of psychology very successfully.

I think our readers would enjoy reading in his book *From Both Ends of the Bench*, how Vernon told what happened immediately before and after that famous timeout.

> *The last few seconds were ticking off the clock in the first overtime of a basketball game between Kentucky and the Temple Owls, a game that had already been tied 16 times. Guy Rodgers (Temple's All American guard), one of the greatest basketball players of all time, was putting on a one man show dribbling and freezing out the clock, with 41 seconds left and the score tied at 69 - 69. There was nothing we could do short of fouling, and we certainly didn't want to do that and just hand them the game. With three seconds left, Rodgers hit a*

short jump shot making the score 71 to 69 for Temple. We managed to stop the clock with one second left.

Coach Rupp said that now they would expect us to throw a long pass to someone under the basket. He said, "Crigler, you take the ball out of bounds. Hatton, you stand close to him, line yourself up with the basket and get a good shot off." Coach Rupp actually felt that we were still in the game and stood there, calm as a Judge, giving us our final instructions. His optimism must have rubbed off on me, because I felt confident that I could make the shot.

Crigler threw me the ball low, so I could make a continuous sweep toward the basket with plenty of leverage. I shot a two-handed shot from 47 feet, and truthfully, I thought it was good all the way. The score was now tied at 71 - 71 with the second overtime coming up. At the end of the second overtime it was tied 75 - 75, and at the end of the third overtime, we had squeaked out an 85 - 83 victory.

It sometimes happens that after a player has such a dramatic part in winning a close game, the coach will honor that player by presenting him the game ball. Hatton was aware of that policy and he felt like he had earned that game ball, so he paid the coach a visit.

"Coach would you give me the game ball from last night?"

Give you the game ball? Just because you scored two points from 47 feet with one second to go, you want me to give you the game

*ball? How would I explain that to the Athletic
Board, giving away a $35 basketball? What
would they think of me spending all of that
money? Anyway, if you hadn't scored that basket, it would have been one of the other boys.
It was just one of our plays we have been practicing for occasions like that."*

Vernon was furious and ready to leave the office. Then a
big smile came on Adolph's face as he reached under his desk and
pulled out the game ball and flipped it to Vernon.
"Congratulations, son. You are sure tough in the clutch. You may
have this ball. Tell your grandchildren about it."

The above is a true story and it shows a part of Adolph
Rupp that many people have not seen. I have said many times
that, inside that rough, gruff exterior, was a kind gentleman with
a heart as big as the outdoors who would not hurt a flea unless it
bit him.

That great game is still being talked about, as it will probably continue to be for many more years.

When Coach Rupp called for Vernon to shoot from near
mid-court instead of trying to pass to a player near the basket, it
showed again what an astute coach he was. Most coaches would
have attempted the long pass hoping for a short jump shot.
Adolph was not only a great coach, he was a quick thinker.

December 14, 1958, we played St. Louis there and while
we were there, Coach Rupp tried to encourage Marie to move to
Lexington. We were participants in a post game party in the hotel
room when the subject came up. After a few others had commented on reasons why we should make such a move, Adolph
looked at Marie and said, "Marie, why in the hell don't you and
Doc just go ahead and move to Lexington where you belong? I'll
tell you what - you all move to Lexington and, by God, we will
make you the Belle of the Bluegrass."

With a game like the one just described above, one might
easily suspect that Temple University was our bitterest non-con-

ference opponent. But that assumption is not necessarily true. Back then, St. Louis was somewhat of a thorn to Adolph and many of his followers.

One night in Kiel Auditorium, we were playing St. Louis and the time keeper used a blank pistol instead of a horn to signal time outs and so forth. Coach Ed Hickey's grown son was the time keeper and our coaches were sorta smarting under the skin because of an item in the paper that quoted Coach Hickey as saying, "I know what it takes to beat Kentucky - I have Adolph's number." Well, young Hickey was sitting next to Harry and the first time he fired the pistol it struck Harry's leg. Harry told Hickey about it and asked him to please be more careful. The next shot also struck his leg. That time Harry's attitude had changed somewhat and he said, "You shoot me one more time with that damn gun and I'll knock you on your ass."

Sure enough, the next shot really scorched Harry's leg and he kept his promise. He wheeled and really knocked the hell out of the timekeeper - man and folding chair fell over backward. The police came in a hurry and said they were taking Harry to head-quarters. But Bernie Shively, our 6' 7", 260 pound athletic director intervened and nobody went to the police station.

Not long after the Temple game, a self-styled student-of-basketball stopped Adolph in the hallway one day and asked, "Why do you continue to play that Beck boy when he has shown in game after game he can't score?"

Adolph said, "Neither can his opponents."

We had another overtime game that season on. February 22, 1958, we beat Alabama 45 to 43 in Montgomery, and then let Auburn beat us 64 to 63 two nights later in Birmingham.

About a week before that Alabama game, we played Loyola in Chicago in what was supposed to have been an easy game. However, the team played a miserable first half and Adolph was fit to be tied. It seemed that everything went wrong. In fact, he was so upset he did not go to the dressing room at the end of the half. But just before time to take the floor for the second half, he stuck his head in the door and said, "Oh, excuse me, I didn't know this was the ladies room." Then he went to our bench and let Harry accompany the team. That was another example of his unique psychological ploys. He used a lot of them. I have often said that the man may not have had any formal training in psychology, but he sure was a master of practical psychology and that knowledge certainly helped him to motivate his players. In fact, when it came to motivating players and getting the most out of them, he had no peers.

Another oddity of this team - one which is almost unbelievable, is that it failed to win its own UKIT, losing to a very fine team from West Virginia 77 to 70, December 20, 1957, then later won both the SEC Championship and the National Championship.

Let me tell you about that 1958 NCAA Tournament.

The Midewest Regional was played in Lexington, on March 14 and 15, 1958.

We defeated Miami of Ohio the 14th, 94 to 70 and Notre Dame won their game with ease to set up the Regional Championship between Kentucky and Notre Dame on the 15th. The rumors making the rounds after those two games and also the next day were not only comical but, as proved a few hours later, somewhat ridiculous.

The Notre Dame coach and players were well aware of Kentucky's erratic season and the word got out that instead of preparing for this championship game with Kentucky, they were planning how they were going to play in the NCAA finals the following weekend. As always, Adolph and Harry were getting the Fiddling Five ready to play Notre Dame with not even a hint of playing in Louisville next week.

Well, everyone who saw that game still remembers the outcome, Kentucky 89, "The Fighting Irish" of Notre Dame 56 - a 35 point margin.

We will never know how that game would have come out if Notre Dame had not been so over-confident and had not motivated the Wildcats by publicizing their lack of respect for Kentucky. Those two factors certainly gave our coaches a lot of assistance in motivating the players for that game.

Now that the Fiddling Five was ready to embark on that journey to the Final Four, I think this a good time and place to list the names of those country basketball playing musicians.

Vernon Hatton 6' 3"	Senior guard	17.1 avg. pts.
Johnny Cox 6' 4"	Junior forward	14.9
Ed Beck 6' 7"	Senior center	5.6
Adrian Smith 6' 0"	Senior guard	12.4
John Crigler 6' 3"	Senior forward	13.6

Please notice only one player is as tall as 6 foot 7 inches, and he was the low scorer. However, Ed was such a fine defensive player, his opponents averaged fewer points than he did. Each of the other four averaged in double figures. By all standards, this was a real small team, but one that was superbly coached.

The stage was now set for another appearance in the Final Four. This tournament was scheduled to be played in Freedom Hall in Louisville the same week that the Kentucky High School Tournament would be played in the UK Coliseum in Lexington. We had reservations at the Lafayette Hotel in Lexington for both tournaments - actually for three tournaments in two weekends.

Coach Rupp got our tickets for both UK tournaments. However, Marie knew my brother Herschel (Pond) was quite anxious to see the Final Four, so she gave him her ticket and stayed in Lexington for the high school tournament. Pond and I drove back to Lexington each night after our game. It was more fun staying in Lexington.

Thousands of people were surprised when the drawing placed Kentucky and Temple in the same bracket for a repeat performance of their three overtime game in December.

As expected, this game with Temple was another cliffhanger. The event was nip-and-tuck from start to finish with Temple leading most of the time. As usual, Guy Rodgers was outstanding and played a fantastic game.

With 17 seconds left in the game and Temple leading by

one point, Kentucky called time out.   Adolph called for his favorite play in this situation, the "pick-and-roll" play with the "back-block."   Let me try to explain this play and the way it worked against Temple's defense.

Temple had a big ole center who was rather slow on his feet. The play called for Vernon to drive toward the basket, knowing a fine defensive player would be guarding him but as he crossed the free throw line, Ed Beck was to step out and let Vernon pass him but block out the guard - leaving Temple's big slow center to try to guard Vernon. No contest. Vernon went in for an easy lay-up and two points, giving Kentucky the lead 61 to 60.

Needless to say, that play had been practiced many times before this game. Vernon's basket, of course, gave the ball to Temple with seven seconds left in the game. However, the guard that brought the ball up court made a bad pass that went into the stands, giving the ball - and the game - to Kentucky.

The above brings to mind another feature of Adolph's coaching that helped make him the premier basketball coach of the world. He did not use nearly as many different plays as a lot of coaches do. All of his plays were run from "patterns" (designs on the floor) and practiced over and over - again and again, until each player knew the pattern so well he ran them as if he were reacting to reflex actions and not having to think about them. One SEC coach told me after we had defeated his team rather decisively, "Hell, Doc, we know every play Kentucky runs against us before the game starts, but they run the damn plays so well and with such precision, we cannot stop them."

Also, Coach Rupp didn't use too many fundamental drills, but the ones he did use were used over and over so many times the players ran them automatically and every drill was designed to help run the plays to near perfection. Adolph's philosophy was that anything less than perfect was not good enough and "we need to practice on that a little more."

Eliminating Temple, of course, set us up to play Seattle with the great Elgin Baylor the next night for the NCAA championship.

When Baylor and his teammates man-handled that Kansas basketball team of real giants, they convinced a lot of people they were for real and it would require a most excellent team to defeat them. Needless to say, Seattle was favored to win the championship.

A little "behind-the scenes" planning took place the night before that final game. This is not the time or place to discuss that, but suffice it to say that in trying to prevent Mr. Baylor from getting into foul trouble by guarding such a star as Johnny Cox, the Seattle coach, unaware that John Crigler was a scoring threat with great ability to drive on a guard for lay-up shots, assigned Baylor to guard Crigler. Boy howdy. What a tactical error that was! Crigler was so adapt at driving on his opponent that he lured Baylor into committing three personal fouls the first half. Then, to add insult to injury, Adolph sent in our substitute center, Don Mills, early in the second half and he tricked Baylor into committing his fourth four. That proved to be the end-gate. For all practical purposes, we could have "put the chairs in the wagon then and gone home" - "church was out." The final score was UK 84, Seattle 72.

I still remember very vividly Adolph celebrating and hugging our beautiful cheerleaders. He was a happy man as were many thousands of other Kentuckians from Ashland to the Mississippi River.

Kentucky had just won its fourth NCAA Championship - more than any other school had ever won.

Chicken and
Wild Rice Casserole

4 cups cooked wild rice
4 cups chicken, cooked and diced
2 cups celery, chopped
2 small onions, chopped
1 can mushrooms
2 10-1/2 ounce cans mushroom soup
2 10-1/2 ounce cans cream of chicken soup
2 cups chicken broth
1/4 cup cashew nuts, optional

Combine rice, chicken, celery, onions and mushrooms in a large bowl. In small bowl combine soups and broth; mix into chicken mixture. Place in casserole dish and top with nuts if desired. Bake at 325° for 1 hour.
Serves 12

Note: If brown rice is substituted for wild rice, use only 1 cup broth.

Bernie Shively

Homemade Rolls

2 packages yeast
1/4 cup warm water
1/2 cup sugar
1/2 cup shortening
1 cup warm water
3 beaten eggs
4-1/2 cups flour
2 teaspoons salt

Dissolve yeast in 1/4 cup warm water. Cream sugar and shortening; add 1 cup warm water, eggs and yeast. Stir in flour and salt. Cover and let stand in refrigerator overnight. About three hours before serving, divide into 4 sections. Make each section into a circle on floured board. Cover with melted butter and cut into 6 pie shape pieces. Roll up into crescent rolls. Let rise about 3 hours. Bake at 400° for 10 minutes.
Make 2 dozen.

Vernon Hatton

Caramel-Filled Brownies

1 German chocolate cake mix
3/4 cup butter, melted
1/2 cup evaporated milk
1 package caramels with paper wrappers removed
1/3 cup evaporated milk
1/2 cup pecans, chopped, optional
6 ounces chocolate chips, optional

Mix cake mix, butter and 1/2 cup evaporated milk; spread one half of the mixture into a buttered 9x13" buttered baking dish. Bake for 15 minutes at 350°. Meanwhile melt caramels and 1/3 cup evaporated milk in top of double boiler. Remove cake from oven and pour caramel mixture evenly over the top. Spread pecans and/or chocolate chips over caramel if desired. Spoon rest of chocolate cake mixture over the top, using finger tips to spread out evenly. Bake for an additional 20 minutes. Let cool overnight or put in freezer for an hour and then frost with chocolate icing. Score, cut and decorate each bar with a pecan half, if desired.
Serves 36 to 48.

Adrian Smith

Chapter VI

In 1958 - 59, Kentucky won 24 and lost 3.

Judging this season by the above win - loss record, one would think this was another glorious year. But, oh! What a painful loss that third one was to Louisville in the NCAA Mideast Regional in Evanston, Ill. Mississippi State won the SEC that year but declined the bid. State defeated us in Starkville 66 to 58, February 9, 1959.

Marie and I were in Starkville for that game and the students were so rude to us and were so vulgar, Marie said she would never go there for another game. But she did.

On February 14, 1959, we defeated Notre Dame 71 to 52. Johnny Cox was an All-American and the team captain that year. After the game, Johnny was milling around the lobby there in the Sherman Hotel and I happened to notice he was wearing one of the most dilapidated hats I had seen in a long time. So I asked Harry if it would be alright if I took Johnny in the men's shop and bought him a hat. He said, "Hell no, Doc. If you did that, some son-of-a-bitch would report you to the NCAA and they would declare Johnny ineligible for the rest of the season."

Sid Cohen was benched for that game for disciplinarian

reasons. After we got to the gym we learned that Sid's sister had flown from Philadelphia to see him play. I found out where she was sitting then went to her seat to explain why Sid was not playing. Needless to say, I concocted a "little white lie" by telling her Sid developed a throat infection before leaving Lexington and, since Coach Rupp thought we could win even without Sid, we both agreed it would be unfair for him to play when he was not physically able. When Sid learned what I told his sister, he almost kissed me there in the hotel lobby.

During a period of years of the 1950's and early 1960's, I took a train to Opelika, Alabama, and saw all of our games in Auburn - about four miles from the Opelika railroad station.

In 1959 - 60, the Wildcats won 18, and lost 7.

After the last year's great season, the win-loss record this time did not look so good. However, this season had at least one big plus for Marie and me. After promising Coach Rupp a couple years ago that we would go to Los Angeles for the double-header he was planning we kept that promise and flew out for those two games.

We beat UCLA 68 to 66 on December 4, 1959, but there was no way we could make a clean sweep of that event. Southern California won the second game on December 5th, 87 to 73.

The first day there, while visiting with the coaches in the hotel lobby, "Wah Wah" Jones came in. When he saw us, he said, "Well I'll be damn - I wouldn't believe this if I wasn't seeing it."

A week after our loss to Southern California, Marie and I headed for St. Louis and saw St. Louis beat us 73 to 61, the night of December 12, 1959.

As usual, a few ladies followed the team and were in the hotel lobby when the coaches and players entered. Bless their hearts, they knew the players felt pretty downcast after the game, so they proceeded to offer words of encouragement. As Sid Cohen came in, they started congratulating him on his good game. Adolph heard them and yelled out, "Don't tell him he played a good game when you know damn well he didn't." Boy howdy! It was a rare incident indeed when the coach complimented a player if he thought the player had not earned a compliment. He was not prone to flattery.

Losing a game always hurts, but our wounds received a dose of good healing balm January 5, 1960, when we stuck it to Vanderbilt 76 to 59 in Nashville after beating Ohio State 96 to 93 December 28th in Lexington. NOT A BAD SEASON.

Although we lost to Georgia Tech 62 to 54 on January 2, 1960, I shall never forget the post-game party at the Rupp home. Since that was the day after New Years, Marie stayed home with Mother and Donna, so I was alone. The party was a "honey" and lasted until well after midnight.

Eventually the guests started leaving and finally Harry and Louise Lancaster and I were the only ones left. As we three prepared to leave, Adolph said to Harry, "No, you and Doc are not leaving. We three are going to talk over that game and try to figure out what in the hell happened." Then he went upstairs to their bedroom and came back carrying what appeared to be an ordinary walking cane, but the cane was hollow and filled with bourbon that had been given to him by an official of a distillery. Well, we finally finished "talking over that game" and I got back to the Lafayette Hotel after 3:15 AM.

I was so wide awake I could see no good reason for going to bed at that hour, so I checked out of the hotel and headed for Clinton, some 330 miles away over a crooked two-lane road, arriving home safely about 9:00 AM. That was a night to remember.

Our game with Auburn there February 20, 1960 still sticks pretty deeply in my craw. It was a game that we needed to win to insure getting a bid to the NCAA. The game was very close and we were aware of the fact that the officials were granting Kentucky no favors. With seconds left in the game, we scored and took the lead. Auburn made a floor mistake and we got the ball with 3 seconds left 60 to 59 in our favor. Rupp called time out and gave instructions. He stressed in no uncertain terms NO FOULING.

Well, the ball was passed in to Sid Cohen just as his man sneaked up behind him. Sid turned without looking and was called for charging. Auburn made both free throws and won 61 to 60. When we returned to the dressing room, Sid could not hide his tears. Adolph saw how Sid felt and said, "That was a stupid G__d__ foul and it very probably cost us a bid to the NCAA. But, we would have still won the damn game if some of you others had not played such a horseshit game to put us in that predicament. Get showered and dressed."

We had another streak of bad luck earlier in that same game. Dick Parsons sustained a severe ankle sprain during the first half. We kept his ankle in an ice pack for quite awhile, but he was unable to come close to his usual playing ability again that night. I still like to think what might have happened if Dick had not been injured.

By the time the 1960 - 61 began, Coach Rupp had developed such a habit of being an annual winner and never suffering a losing season, people started asking what he could now do for an encore.

During the summer of 1960, Florida State University offered me a job as team physician for both basketball and football - a very tempting job it was, too. While trying to decide about moving to Florida, Marie came up with an idea that was hard to ignore. She said she had been thinking about something and she thought I should give it some pretty serious consideration. She then said, "Now, just think about this situation for awhile. Suppose you take that job, then next year Florida State is playing Kentucky and you look over at their bench and see your two good friends, Coaches Rupp and Lancaster, how will you feel? I sure would not want you to make such a major change as that and then decide you had made a big mistake. We both know how you feel about Coach Rupp and Harry. They are both unquestionably two of your very best friends." After that mini-lecture, it did not take me long to decide to remain in Clinton, Kentucky, and continue that 330 mile drive to and from Lexington to see our beloved Wildcats play basketball. I never regretted that decision.

The record for 1960-61 was 19 wins, 9 losses.

This seasonal record would be considered successful by many schools and coaches but for Adolph Rupp, it approached being a disaster. Winning only 68% of his games was just not acceptable at all.

After we lost to Marquette 88 to 72 in Chicago, March 11, 1961, the three of us were in Harry's hotel room after the game. Our conversation was of a very serious vein and completely devoid of any thoughts of celebration. The three os us had never made any pretense of being good losers. I doubt if there are such.

Adolph finally broke the ice and said, "Harry, we have got to get some good players for next year with at least one big man who can play. Do you have any suggestions?"

Harry teasingly said, "Well, Adolph, between the two of us, we have better than a million dollars and we can spend some of that money on recruiting. But, there is a hitch. I just have about fifty dollars and you have all the rest of it." That brought the recruiting talk to a quick halt.

We were woefully weak at the center position this year. Our center was a fine gentleman and had good size but he was not quick enough to really compete with several of the opponents who faced him. St. Louis beat us in the UKIT final game 74 to 72 in overtime. Then on March 18, 1961, Ohio State and Jerry Lucas eliminated us in the NCAA Mideast Regional in Louisville 87 to 74. We had erased Morehead 71 to 64 the night before. They had a weak center, too.

Soon after that embarrassing game with Ohio State came to an end, Coach Rupp and I were in the men's room of our locker room when a little redheaded reporter came in to interview the coach. He had never known Adolph before and knew nothing of the man's mannerisms_especially after suffering such an embarrassing and frustrating defeat.

The reporter asked Adolph, "Coach, what would you say was the turning point in that game?"

"Turning point?" Rupp answered. "I'll tell you what the

turning point was _ it was that G__d___ 6' - 8" player of ours who tried to be center."

The reporter looked like he was scared out of his wits. He made a feeble attempt at thanking Adolph as he was leaving and we didn't see him again, nor did we see his report in the papers later.

The 1961 - 62 team won 23 and lost 3.

Although we lost three starters, the center and both forwards, from last year's team, prospects for a better season were looking up. Cotton Nash, a 6' - 5" sophomore center - forward who was one of the nation's most highly recruited high school seniors two years before, was a sure starter. Also, we had three other excellent shooters and a fifth man who was a top-notch defensive player.

There were so many ridiculous and, at times, insulting incidents during our games in Starkville with Mississippi State during the 1950's and 1960's, I cannot be sure just which year some of them happened. However, I want to mention one.

This particular night, a young man whom we thought was a student, sat on the front row of the side seats, close to and opposite our bench which was at the end of the court. He had a loud megaphone with which he harassed Coach Rupp with the most insulting and vulgar language I have ever heard in public. To make matters worse, we recognized some Mississippi faculty members and security officers within easy ear-shot of that man and not one time did any of the officials attempt to quiet him down. But to top it all, when we returned from the dressing room to start the second half, someone had left the skin of a skunk under Coach Rupp's chair!

Although this was a wonderful season for our win-loss record, we swallowed a bitter pill in the NCAA Mideast Regional on March 17, 1962 when Ohio State again defeated us in the final game 74 to 64, this time in Iowa City, Iowa.

The 1962 - 63 squad won 16 and lost 9.

This season was not one of our best ones; however, it did have some very interesting incidents for Marie and me which were also related to Coach Rupp.

For several years during the 1950's and 60's, the *Paducah Sun* newspaper sponsored an annual banquet the last of October for basketball coaches, fans and members of the media.

One year, Coach Adolph Rupp was the guest speaker and I was an invited guest. When the coach was introduced, the capacity crowd gave him a standing ovation. He responded by saying, "Thank you so much for that wonderful ovation, I appreciate that. In fact, I think the audience should always give the speaker a standing ovation when he is introduced. I don't know what that does for the ladies, but it gives the men a chance to straighten their shorts." The mixed crowd really applauded those remarks.

This was also Sam Harper's second year at UK. Sam was from our home town of Clinton and, due to circumstances beyond his control, Adolph could not make the trip to sign Sam to the basketball scholarship the day he was due to do so. So he called me and asked me to sign Sam for him, which I did. I just happened to have a blank form or two for that purpose.

The first game I remember was at Northwestern on December 7, 1963. We won it 95 to 63 but the game was not the only excitement that day.

I went to Evanston via train and arrived at the hotel at noon. The coaches and "followers" were in the dinning room and when Adolph saw me, he motioned me to his table. He was quite anxious to get his blood pressure checked. After lunch his blood pressure was pretty high, so I gave him a tablet for it.

During the game that night, he got to feeling pretty bad and when the game was over we got Bob Lutes to take him to the hotel instead of to the dressing room.

Back in his hotel room Adolph said, "Doc, you come to all of our games, so from now on I want you to sit right behind me at our bench. Will you do it?" That was the beginning of my sitting behind that vacant chair that was always between Adolph and Harry - and listening intently to their conversations during the games.

The day of the game with Northwestern the Evanston paper stated rather emphatically that the Kentucky Wildcats were in town to "try to play" with Northwestern. The writer was of the opinion that the game would, in all probability, develop into teaching the basic fundamentals of basketball to the boys from Kentucky. Apparently, that sports writer knew nothing about Kentucky basketball and even less about Randy Embry as a play maker.

Randy had a way of school-hopping as he leisurely brought the ball up-court and on this night, such antics seemed to upset the Northwestern defense. It must have really done so because, we won the game 95 to 63, a margin of 32 points.

The next morning the same writer said, "The University of Kentucky taught Northwestern last night how the game of basketball should be played." Since this game was played December 7, 1964, the results made it a fitting anniversary for the Pearl Harbor disaster of December 7, 1941.

When the schedule was officially published, it listed our game with Ole Miss in Jackson, Mississippi on Saturday, February 9, 1963. Jackson just happens to be on the Illinois Central Railroad, the same as Clinton, KY. So a group of UK fans from Clinton chartered a private railroad car for the round trip to Jackson to see our "hometown boy" play.

While sitting around the afternoon of the game, J.D. Reeves came by and gave a "paper sack" of cooked quail to Adolph. There were too many quail for one man to eat, so I helped out by eating a fair share of them.

Later during the afternoon, Harry reminded me we were playing Mississippi State the following Monday night in Starkville and suggested I fly there with the team on Sunday. I did and after we arrived in Columbus where we were staying, I called Marie and asked her to drive down for the game. Bless her heart, she did and had to drive over icy roads for a number of miles.

Adolph had commented a number of times in the past about my eating such big breakfasts and never gaining weight. For breakfast that morning in the Holiday Inn Restaurant, they served unusually good bacon but not enough for me, so I ordered an additional order of bacon. Just as the waitress brought the order, Adolph sat down beside me. His remark was, "How in the hell can you eat so damn much bacon and never gain an ounce?"

Harry knew I had given Adolph a pretty strong sedative the night before and asked him how he slept. He answered, "Very little, not a wink until well after two o'clock."

Harry then asked him, "Did the storm keep you awake?"

"Storm - what storm?" Seems he had slept through the whole thunderstorm.

Cotton Nash had not played too well against State before this and Adolph asked me to talk to him and maybe encourage him to play a little better. Well, Cotton and I had a good visit that day but we still lost the game 56 to 52. It was hard for us to beat Babe McCarthy's teams on their floor.

In compiling that record, UK easily won its UKIT by defeating Wisconsin 108 to 85 and Wake Forest 98 to 75 in the final game.

That final game was an extra plus for me. I attended Wake Forest Medical School for two years before transferring to University of Louisville School of Medicine. At the end of my sophomore year, I was awarded a Bachelor of Science degree.

Also, the colorful coach of Wake Forest really put on a spectacular exhibition of showmanship to add to the entertainment. He was noted for wearing bright red socks and managed to exhibit them every chance he could by keeping his pant legs a few inches above his ankles. Needless to say, "Bones," as he was affectionately called, pulled off a few other comical tricks. I think Coach Rupp enjoyed his showmanship as much as any of the fans.

This team also won the Sugar Bowl by defeating Loyola (La) 86 to 64 and Duke 81 to 79.

I shall long remember that Duke game. Jeff Mullins, a

graduate of Lafayette High School, in Lexington, was Duke's high scoring, All-American guard. We all knew that Larry Conley was the most likely man to to guard Mullins.

While Harry, one of the assistant coaches, and I were eating dinner a few hours before the game, the subject of guarding Jeff was discussed. After listening to the other two awhile, I asked Harry, "Do you think Tommy might be more able to handle Jeff than Larry?"

Harry glared at me with a big frown and said, "Doc, you think Kron can guard Mullins better than Larry can, don't you? Tell me, why do you think that?"

I said, "Well, Tommy is a very quick, strong 6' - 5"guard, an inch taller than Jeff and a helluva lot stronger that Larry. I really think he is the best guard we have against a player like Jeff."

Harry said, "You just may have something there."

The assistant coach said, "Harry, I agree with Doc."

By the time the first half was half over, it was evident that Larry could not guard Jeff. So a little later Harry nudged Adolph and said, "Get Larry out." He did and without another word to Coach Rupp, Harry yelled out, "Tommy get in there and guard Mullins." Mullins scored one more basket that half and had a miserable second half against Tommy. Tommy was a starting guard after that game.

Governor Happy Chandler was sitting in the front row just a short distance from the end of our bench and he kept trying to frustrate Mullins by yelling, "Mullins, when we get back to Lexington, we are going to revoke your Kentucky citizenship. We are going to disenfranchise you." It's sorta hard to know which Adolph enjoyed more, Kron's guarding Mullins or Happy's harassment of Mullins. I think both helped us win the game.

After we returned to the hotel, Adolph asked our trainer and me to go with him to the Pearl Oyster and Shrimp Bar. We all ordered shrimp. Joe was not at all accustomed to eating shrimp as soon as you peel them, and was "stockpiling" his. What he didn't notice was Adolph and me snitching shrimp from his plate. When he finally did realize it, we were just about finished with our meal and, although he had eaten only a few bites, most of his food was gone. He told us most emphatically that was the last time he would ever go out with us.

The season was still young. We went on to lose three SEC games, and to get upset later by St. Louis at home after winning the SEC championship.

The NCAA Mideast Regional Tournament was in Minneapolis, Minn. Our first opponent was Ohio University and we were favored by 22 points. However, we had a most strange situation this year. Our very fine All-American senior forward had been known to have a few miserable games and I had learned by watching him very closely during the pre-game warmups to predict pretty accurately when he was in for a bad game. So during warmup before our game with Ohio University, I told our trainer we were in trouble. He wanted to know why I thought so. I said just watch - real carefully. He is not going to play well at all, just like at Mississippi State. This player averaged 24 points this year. At the end of the half he had 2 points and we were several points behind. For the game, he scored a total of 5 points and we lost by 16 points, 85 to 69.

During the previous two years, I had observed that this otherwise great forward just couldn't produce when he most wanted to. This night he was especially anxious to play well because he knew the pro scouts were there to evaluate him.

After the game, I was sitting alone in the hotel lobby when Adolph and Esther came through. He stopped and asked "What are you doing Doc?"

I said "Nothing - just nothing."

He said "Come on up to the room with us - I want to talk to you." After we got settled and he poured a couple of drinks, he looked at me and said, "Doc, what in the hell do you think happened tonight?"

I said, "The record shows our All-American forward was a flop."

"Hell, he got nothing done but why?"

I said, "Adolph, when I say what's on my mind, you may

want to make me walk home but I'm going to speak my mind anyway. As you well know, when he really wants to turn it on and make a show, the pressure gets to him like a case of very severe stage fright and he simply cannot play under all of that pressure. Now you probably will disagree with me but I have been wanting to say this for a long time. Regardless of how you now feel about Al Groza, he always seemed to play his best games under pressure. In fact, he had no bad games."

Coach Rupp said, "Hell Doc, this guy couldn't carry Al's jock-strap." That was the first time I had heard Adolph call Al's name since the so-called scandal of 1948 - 49. I was present the next time he saw Al. They shook hands and had a very friendly visit.

Losing that game really shook our team's morale and the next night, we lost the consolation game to Loyola (Chicago) 100 to 91.

Wah Wah's Cole Slaw

1/3 cup milk
4 tablespoons vinegar
2 tablespoons sugar
3 tablespoons water
1/4 cup commercial slaw dressing
1/4 cup green pepper, grated
1/2 cup carrot, grated
1/2 teaspoon onion, grated
1/2 head cabbage, grated

In a small bowl mix milk, vinegar, sugar, water and slaw dressing. In medium bowl mix green pepper, carrot, onion and cabbage. Pour dressing over vegetables and toss. Refrigerate for at least one hour before serving.

Wah Wah Jones

Heavenly Apple Salad

1 3-ounce package lemon gelatin
1 3-ounce package lime gelatin
2 cups hot water
1 cup cold water
1 13-ounce can crushed pineapple
2 large apples, diced
1/2 cup walnuts or pecans, chopped
1/2 cup sugar
2 tablespoons lemon juice
2 eggs, beaten
1 cup whipping cream, whipped

Dissolve gelatins in hot water. Stir in cold water; chill until mixture is semi-firm. Add apples, drained pineapple and nuts. Chill until firm. Beat together sugar, lemon juice and eggs. Cook until thickened. Cool thoroughly. Fold in whipped cream. Spread on salad. Refrigerate until chilled then cut and serve on bed of lettuce.

Dick Parsons

Cream of Bluegrass Pie

1 cup milk, scalded
1/4 cup flour
1/3 cup sugar
1/8 teaspoon salt
1 egg, beaten
1/4 teaspoon vanilla, lemon or orange extract
1 Nine inch baked pie shell
1/2 cup red currant jelly, melted
1-1/2 cups fresh blueberries, rinsed and drained or
1 10-ounce package frozen blueberries

In a small bowl mix flour, sugar, salt and egg; stir in 1/4 cup of the hot milk. Return to double boiler. Cook and stir until the mixture thickens. Continue to cook 5 minutes longer. Cool covered; add vanilla, lemon or orange extract. Spread in pie shell. Add 1/2 tablespoon hot water to the jelly; stir with a fork or small whisk and melt in a double boiler. Add the blueberries. Spread over the cream filling. Chill and serve the day it is made.

Note: Cool the custard and the blueberry mixture before uniting them as it prevents sweating and keeps them from separating when the pie is cut.

Cotton Nash

Chapter VII

The 1964 - 65 record shows 15 wins, 10 losses.

Although this year was not one of Coach Rupp's best seasons by any means, it was much more important to my family and me. This would be our last year to drive 330 miles from Clinton, to Lexington to attend our home games.

I had been hoping we would move to Lexington sometime, but we didn't actually make any definite plans for such a move until around the first of the year. However, once we made a decision, plans developed quite rapidly.

It was in Lexington the weekend of October 16th - 18th, 1964, presumably for a football game. However, my primary purpose was to see a new, small shopping center on Bryan Station Road. A drug salesman and good friend of mine told me at the annual meeting of the Kentucky Medical Association in Louisville a few days before that if I was ever going to move to Lexington, this shopping center would be a perfect location for me.

On the way home Sunday, a pain developed in the right side of my back. To make a long story short, the next day the pain was so bad that I left the office at 4:00 PM. I went home and was later transferred to Baptist Hospital in Memphis. Dr. Harwell

Wilson, Professor of Surgery at University of Tennessee Medical Center and a close personal friend, did my appendectomy about midnight, Monday. Everything went fine until Thursday morning when I awoke with left chest pains and a temperature of 101 degrees. A few hours later, I was unconscious and remained so for five days. I stayed in the hospital a total of twenty-two days due to a left pulmonary embolus.

Coach Rupp learned of my condition and called Marie every day to check on me. But he did another thing that we appreciated even more, and one that we shall never forget. Donna's birthday was November 2nd and she was in school at UK. Coach Rupp sent her a dozen red roses and took the basketball team to her dormitory to wish her a Happy Birthday and to assure her that her Daddy was going to be alright. She called Marie at the hospital that night and said under the circumstances, she believed that was the best birthday present she had ever gotten.

After seeing the Hi Acres Shopping Center and talking to some people in the area, I was convinced the place was really tailor-made for the type of practice I wanted. I was cognizant of the fact that I was nearing the age when I should discontinue the practice of major surgery and obstetrics. Also I realized that making such a major change in my professional life-style would most certainly be somewhat of a traumatic one. However, being located in an area somewhat inconvenient for hospital practice would probably make the transition much less painful for both Marie and me.

In that respect, the geographical location of Hi Acres was ideal.

While in Lexington the weekend of October 16 - 18, 1964, I talked to Mr. A.P. Schneider about building me an office for me. He assured me that would pose no problem.

When we left the hospital in Memphis, the doctors urged me to continue taking coumandin for at least two years to prevent any additional blood clots. However, soon after returning home, my physical "well-being" improved remarkably, but it was only a relatively short time until I was stricken with a another disease -

"basketball fever."

On December 18, 1964, I drove alone to Lexington for the UKIT, knowing full well an accident with only minor lacerations could be fatal. After returning home, I made out a schedule for gradually discontinuing the coumandin and periodically checking my bleeding and clotting time.

On my next trip to Lexington, in January, 1965, I made tentative arrangements for Mr. Schneider to build that office. He told me to draw the floor plans the way I wanted the office arranged and he would start the building as soon as the weather permitted.

By this time I had regained my strength and endurance sufficiently to drive and see a few office patients, but I certainly was not physically able to assume the practice of general surgery or obstetrics again. However, a little later, I let two of my former patients inveigle me into doing their cesarean sections. Fortunately, their delivery dates were approximately a week apart. But after each of those operations, I was so completely exhausted it was necessary to rest on the cot in the doctors' dressing room for 30 or 40 minutes before dressing in street clothes.

Since the above two operations were easy to do but each procedure was so tiring for me, I realized that I should retire from the practice of general surgery and obstetrics and perhaps limit my practice to office work. But such limitations to one's practice in a small town is something the general public is most reluctant to accept.

Since moving to Lexington would represent a major change in our lives, it would be unthinkable unless Marie was in complete agreement with me. Needless to say, we had many long discussions and did a lot of praying before making a decision. Once the decision was made, we started making definite plans immediately to move.

On May 20, 1965, I left for Lexington with the moving van and our belongings. Four days later, after I had the apartment and office partially presentable, Marie and Sparkle arrived.

On May 27, 1965, at 9:00 AM we opened the office at

1806 Bryan Station Road, the office that Mr. Schneider had built, and the first patient walked in at 9:05 AM. We were in business.

It didn't take Marie very long to become a true Lexingtonian, not a native of Lexington, but a solid citizen of this wonderful city and a citizen of the Bluegrass. Later, I dubbed the area as "The Land of Milk and Honey" and still frequently refer to it as such.

Coach and Esther Rupp really went out of their way to make us feel at home and especially to keep Marie from getting home sick. The second Saturday we were here, Adolph asked us to go with them to the Trots at the Red Mile race track.

That was our first time at the Red Mile and we really enjoyed it. When all the ladies went to the powder room, Adolph told me, "Doc, we are going to keep Marie so damn busy she won't have time to get homesick."

Our practice started out quite well and slowly increased week by week.

Without our knowledge, Esther started looking for a permanent home for us. She and Adolph both more or less insisted we live in south Lexington, but since the office was in the northeast part of the city, I explained to them it would be much more convenient for us to live in the general area. His retort was, "Hell Doc, people who live in New York commute forty miles each way."

I said, "Yes, but we don't live in New York and those folks in New York don't have to return to the office for emergencies."

We were fortunate to find a real nice building lot in a good residential area and started building in July of 1965. In October we moved into our new home, four days after basketball practice started.

Our first dinner guests were the Rupps. When they reached the front entrance, Adolph looked around and said, "Doc, you have a flat roof?"

"Yes," I said. "We started out with a hip-roof but the mortgage got so heavy it just flattened the thing right out."

Rupp answered, "Oh, I feel so sorry for you damn doctors." And he went right in the house.

Just a short time after practice started in mid October, Russell Rice, who was a sports writer for the *Lexington Leader*, sat with Adolph and me and heard us talking about injuries and treatment and so forth. In his story a day or so later, he mentioned that I was the new basketball team physician.

Our records will show that my practice doubled within two weeks after the story appeared in the *Lexington Leader*. That was one indication of the tremendous influence Coach Rupp and his basketball program had on this community.

My practice got off to such a good start that Marie, Donna and I went to Atlantic City in June to attend the annual meeting of the American Medical Association. I had attended this meeting every year since 1948.

A week after school opened at UK in September, 1965, an official at the UK Medical Center called and offered me a full-time position as a physician in the student section. However, our practice was such then that I felt we would be better off if I continued in private practice - a decision I never regretted.

In 1965 - 66, the UK team won 32, and only lost 2.

In October, 1965, a few days after basketball practice started, three men from Falmouth, Kentucky, paid me a visit _the County Judge, the Hospital Administrator and the Superintendent of Schools. The purpose of their visit was to ask me to move to Falmouth and practice general surgery. The had only three general practitioners and none of them were surgeons.

I thanked the gentlemen for complimenting me with their flattering offer and explained to them why I could not accept it.

A few days later a similar offer to change locations was made by committees from two other towns which had new hospitals but no surgeons.

By this time my infantile practice was doing so well, we both wanted very much to stay in Lexington and had already transferred our church membership to Parkway Baptist Church.

After basketball practice got underway, I left the office at 3:00 PM every day and went to practice.

Several weeks after the first game this team became known as "The Rupp Runts" because of their size. I think it was the smallest major college team I have ever seen. Here is the lineup:

Pat Riley, 6' - 4"	Forward
Larry Conley, 6' - 3"	Forward
Thad Jaracz, 6' - 5"	Center
Louie Dampier, 6' - 0"	Guard
Tommy Kron, 6' - 5"	Guard

I want to mention here an incident that shows what an astute judge of raw basketball talent Coach Rupp was.

When Thad Jaracz was a high school senior, most people thought of him as being no better than average. However, since he lived and went to school in Lexington, Adolph decided he should at least take a look at him. So during Thad's last semester, Adolph and Harry watched him play a game.

After the game, Adolph said, "Harry, I can't quite put my finger on it, but By God, I saw something in that Jaracz kid that I like and I'm going to give him a scholarship."

Before this season was very old, Thad showed a lot of people what Coach Rupp apparently saw in him two years earlier.

Coach Rupp had a fantastic ability for judging a basketball player by watching him play only a game or two.

This was the first team for which I was the official team physician and I learned to love those kids as if they were my sons. Going to practice every day and then watching those "Runts" beat much bigger teams was one of the most gratifying experiences I had ever had.

The last day of practice before our first game, Adolph knew Marie was out of town and he asked me to go home with him for dinner after practice. Soon after we got settled in the living room, he looked at me and said, "Doc, what do you think of this team?"

"Coach," I said, "I think this is going to be one helluva team that will really surprise a lot of coaches."

Adolph answered, "Yea, damn you, you think we are going to win the SEC Championship, don't you?"

"Yes, I do."

"Just how in the hell do you think that when our biggest player in only 6 '- 5"

After I gave my reasons for my optimism, I realized then that he agreed with me but, he did not say so. By this time, we understood each other pretty well. Quite some time later, Harry told me he believed I understood Adolph better than any living person except Esther. Then he added, "And I'm not too sure you don't have her beat."

In addition to it being my first game as team physician, our first game that year on December 1, 1965, was with Hardin-Simmons which was an added thrill for me because my father's first cousin was the president of that school many years before.

During that game, Mr. Bernie (Shive) Shively told me he wanted to talk to me when I had time for him. The next day, December 2, 1965, I went to his office and he really surprised me. Just out of the clear sky, he looked at me and said, "Do you want to be the team doctor for our basketball team?"

I answered him, "Shive, I had rather be the team doctor than president of the university."

He stood up to shake my hand and said, "As of right now, you are the official team physician for the University of Kentucky basketball team." I served as team physician for 17 years, until the end of 1981 - 82 season. Shive and I remained very close friends until his death on December 10, 1967.

The 1965 - 66 season was nothing less that phenomenal. For that team of undersized kids to run rough-shod over such outstanding teams as those on our schedule was unbelievable. Of course, Hardin-Simmons was not expected to win but look at a few of the others.

1965 - 66 Schedule

UK   Opponent

December 1	Hardin-Simmons	(H)	83	55
December 4	Virginia	(A)	99	73
December 8	Illinois	(A)	86	68
December 11	Northwestern	(H)	86	75

UKIT

December 17	Air Force		78	58
December 18	Indiana (finals)		91	56
December 22	Texas Tech	(A)	89	73
December 29	Notre Dame	(H)	103	69
January 3	St. Louis	(H)	80	70
January 8	Florida	(A)	78	64
January 10	Georgia	(A)	69	65
January 15	Vanderbilt	(H)	96	83
January 24	LSU	(H)	111	85
January 29	Auburn	(H)	115	78
January 31	Alabama	(H)	82	62

February 2	Vanderbilt	(A)	105	90
February 5	Georgia	(A)	74	50
February 7	Florida	(H)	85	75
February 12	Auburn	(A)	77	64
February 14	Alabama	(A)	90	67
February 19	Miss State	(A)	73	69
February 21	Mississippi	(A)	108	65
February 26	Tennessee	(H)	78	64
March 5	Tennessee	(A)	62	69
March 7	Tulane	(H)	103	74

During the Tennessee game, Louie missed a few shots from the baseline in the first half because his opponent was getting to him and causing Louie to rush his shots. During the intermission between the halves, Adolph said, "Louie, you are standing like this and when the ball gets to you and you turn to shoot, that son-of-a bitch is on top of you. Now stand like this (he demonstrated) and you can get that shot off before he can get to you and you can make those shots."

I watched Louie very carefully the second half. He took 7 shots from that position and made 6, another demonstration of superb coaching which made a tremendous difference.

Let me say that just before the season of 1965 - 66 opened, this team of "Runts" was not rated in the "top 40" college teams of the nation. However, we won seven games before Christmas, including the UKIT by defeating the Air Force 78 to 58 the first night and Indiana 91 to 56 in the championship game the following night.

We went home to Clinton for the Christmas Holidays and one of the first people I saw was Earl Sensing, the editor of our hometown paper, *The Hickman County Gazette*. Earl was quite anxious for some first-hand news about "that Kentucky team," and asked, "Are they for real?"

I assured him the team not only was for real, but if all the players stayed healthy, they would surprise a lot of people by winning the SEC Championship. I really believed that whole-heartedly. Being a graduate and former sports information director of Murray State, Earl was quite skeptical of my evaluation of the team. But after watching those kids man-handle the bigger teams so decisively and seeing their enthusiasm in practice every day,it was almost impossible for anyone to dampen my outlook. In fact, I was ready to get back to Lexington the next day, but I had to stay awhile longer so I missed a day or two of practice.

Our next game was Saturday, December 22, 1964, at Texas Tech. We won 89 to 73 but the game came very close to being a disaster. Louie Dampier suffered such a severely sprained ankle that X-rays were required to determine that his ankle was not fractured. The trainer and I spent several hours Sunday and Monday trying to speed up Louie's recovery. By practice time Tuesday, Louie was able to slowly jog around the basketball court. When it was time for the team to scrimmage, it happened. Coach Rupp came to the bench where I was sitting and said rather gruffly, "Can Louie scrimmage?"

"No," I said, "he can't coach."

"G__d__ it, Doc, I want him to scrimmage today so he will be ready to play against Notre Dame Saturday. Damn it Doc, you get that ankle well; I can't build a team around a kid sitting on that damn bench with you." Rupp was gone to the far side of the court before I could answer. Frankly I did not have a retort for that last onslaught.

At the time, it never occurred to me that our little first confrontation would make waves outside of the "basketball family." However, the following Saturday a group of Lexington doctors met at St. Joseph Hospital to examine high school football players for spring practice. While I was there, Dr. Ralph Angelucci, a very good friend, walked up to me, placed his arm around my shoulder and said,"V.A., I heard about your little run-in with Adolph the other day. Stay in there, my friend. You are the only doctor we have ever had out there that he couldn't push around." At that time, Ralph was Chairman of the UK Board of Trustees. I was to learn later that "standing my ground" that Tuesday afternoon greatly increased Adolph's confidence in me as a team physician and it relieved him of trying to make medical decisions he was not qualified to make. I'm sure the fact that Louie played against Notre Dame in Louisville on December 29th and that we won 103 to 69 helped my cause. That's right. We beat those rascals 34 points, and they were BIG rascals, too.

Another psychological motivating remark by coach was in a hard scrimmage when Tommy Porter, an All-State 6 '- 4" forward from Hopkinsville and a truly fine basketball player, was playing opposite Pat Riley and was called for offensive goal tending. Needless to say, it displeased the coach but he did not show his feelings until Tommy made the same mistake the third time. Then Adolph stopped the play and yelled out, "Porter, do they have a funeral home in Hopkinsville?"

"Yes Sir, coach, we have three."

"Well by God, you tend goal one more time today and they will need one of them tomorrow."

The night before our home game with St. Louis, Adolph, Harry, the new assistant, Coach Joe B. Hall and I went to Louisville to watch St. Louis play Louisville. St. Louis had a big powerful team. On the way home, Adolph said, "I just don't see any way for us to beat that big bunch of bastards. What do you think Harry?" Harry and Joe both agreed it would be a tough game. Finally, Rupp said, "Doc, you are mighty quiet back there - what do you think?"

I said, "After watching them play, I don't see any way that gang of giants can beat us." We drove a few miles before the conversation was resumed. Fortunately for me, we won that game

January 3rd, 1966, 80 to 70.

Coaches seem to have a tendency for expressing pessimism prior to a big game.

A week after the St. Louis game January 10, 1966, we had a very, very close game at Georgia. The strangest part of that game came rather late when we were in real foul trouble. Freshmen did not play varsity ball then. We had a big 6' - 8" very inexperienced sophomore, Cliff Berger, who had practically no varsity playing time and the Georgia Coach knew that. When Cliff entered the game, Georgia immediately fouled him four times trying to get the ball before we scored. To everyone's surprise, Cliff hit his free throws four times without a miss. We won 69 to 65 in two over-times. On February 5, we beat the same team 74 to 50.

That Georgia game was our only overtime game that year. In fact, it was our only close SEC game. However, a week after we defeated Tennessee 78 to 64 in Lexington, we played there in Knoxville, March 5, 1966. The closer the game time approached, the more misgivings I had concerning the outcome. Even the people in Knoxville had developed a feeling of affection for "Rupp Runts", and they were very open and frank to let us know that since we had already won the conference they were hoping we could finish the season undefeated. I still feel that created an adverse effect on the players and I am equally sure the fans of Tennessee did not intend it that way. They were really for the Wildcats that one time.

But as the record book shows, we did not play well and were defeated 69 to 62.

By this time, Adolph had learned that I limited my drinking to only one drink - regardless of the circumstances. One night during a little stag party in a hotel room after I declined a second drink, he looked at me and said, "Ole one drink Doc." Needless to say, that was his favorite nickname for me from then on.

During the latter part of this 1965 - 66 season, Shive was in my office and casually asked if I knew how much Adolph was advertising me. His question really surprised me. He said, "Doc, he never misses a chance to recommend you. If he hears someone mention high blood pressure or even feeling bad, he will say, 'Hell, if you're sick, why don't you go see Dr. Jackson - he can really fix you up.'"

The NCAA Mideast tournament was played in Iowa City, Iowa March 11 and 12, 1966. Our first game was with Dayton and their 7 ' center. As he had done so consistently all season, Pat Riley, who was only 6' - 4", out jumped the seven footer and got the tip every time. We won that game 86 to 79.

Our opponent in the championship game the next night was University of Michigan. Their bread and butter man was Cassie Russell, a 6' - 5" giant guard who was rated by a lot of people as the number one guard in the USA. Michigan also had a very imposing front line of big players. However, our little "Rupp Runts" feared no basketball team regardless of the awesome size of the players and they took the fight to these giants and won the Mideast Regional 84 to 77.

Kentucky had been rated #1 in the nation since about the second week in January. But, as we all know, there are always a few "Doubting Thomases" who want to be different. Just a couple of days before the tournament opened, a sports writer in Chicago wrote a very sarcastic story about "that Kentucky team being rated the top team in the nation." Then he finished his story with this caustic closure, "Number one basketball team in the nation with no player taller than six - five and no black players? Forget it."

The next day after we won the tournament, that same writer wrote a post-game story in which he said, "I could not believe it was possible for that team of small, white players from Lexington, Kentucky to defeat such a team as Michigan but they did and they also convinced me they have earned their rating as the nation's number one collegiate basketball team."

These were glorious days indeed for the University of Kentucky basketball program but later it seemed that destiny was to provide such an insurmountable obstacle as to prevent this great team from reaching its final goal.

The first night after our triumphant return from Iowa

City, I was called to the players' dormitory because four of them were sick. Although medication was started that night and the players stayed in bed two days, they did not respond as well as we had hoped. Needless to say, practice was curtailed somewhat which added to our woes. We were scheduled to play Duke University, the No. 2 team in the nation, in the NCAA semi-final game Friday, March 18, 1966.

I sent out and got malted milks for some of the players to drink between the halves. One player said after the game he could not have lasted through the second half without that malted milk.

As soon as the players finished their post-game meal they were put to bed and I examined them immediately. Their temperatures were 101 degrees.

When I returned to the hotel lobby, Dr Ralph Angelucci asked about the players' condition. I told him that nothing seemed to be helping very much and the drug I wanted to use had sometimes caused very serious side effects. He said, "Use it V.A., and I promise you the University will stand behind you." I had to go eight miles to the nearest hospital to get the medication in the injectable form. I didn't want to give oral medication for fear of causing upset stomachs.

In their rooms at 2:00 AM, I gave each player the injection in their buttocks. By breakfast time, all three players had normal temperatures but none felt like playing. Still all of them insisted on doing so since we had no substitutes that were their equal.

Pat Riley awoke that morning with an infected foot that was so painful he could hardly walk. When we started to the gym that night, Pat's foot was still so swollen he could not lace his dress shoe.

Pat certainly should not have played that night but he did his best. His field goal percentage for that game dropped 32% below his season average. He could not jump sufficiently to make his usual jump shots.

This little treatise was put in here to show why the nation's number one basketball team in 1965 - 66 did not win the

National Championship.

If we had played Texas Western the first night, we would have won by several points but Duke would have defeated us the second night. Our players were too weakened by illness to play their usual game.

Texas Western won that championship with the help of an illness that the best team could not overcome.

The record book shows that Texas Western defeated University of Kentucky 72 to 65 but it does not say why!

Coach Adolph Rupp and his great assistant coach Harry Lancaster certainly did a super, super job of coaching a great group of kids and actually had them ready to win a well earned National Championship when illness struck. And that team was not rated in the top 40 when the season opened approximately 3 1/2 months earlier.

When I entered our locker room after the game, Louie Dampier was standing in a back corner, crying like a whipped child. I went to Louie to try to offer some comfort but instead of accomplishing that, I just put my arms around him and joined in the "boo-hooing." Mr. Shively, our wonderful Athletic Director, came in and joined us - then there were three weepers, all three crying.

That was only my second time to cry because of losing a basketball game. The only other time was my senior year in high school when Paducah Tilghman High School actually stole a game from us in the Regional Tournament which was played on Tilghman's floor. That night, my crying partner was my brother, Herschel, who was our center while I was a guard and team captain.

During the summer of 1966, Adolph, Harry and Shive took the team to Tel Aviv, Israel to play in the International Universities Tournament.

I shall never forget what Adolph told me at the railroad depot just a few minutes before he boarded the train. He knew I was not going and apparently felt he should be the one to break the news to me.

Claud Sullivan, our beloved radio announcer, had just returned from the Mayo Clinic where he had been because of serious throat trouble. His case had been diagnosed as advanced malignancy of the throat. Adolph said, "It's all over, Doc. There is no hope for recovery." He then boarded the train.

I received a picture postcard from Louie Dampier while they were gone and I still have it.

Harry later told me of an incident abroad in the dining room one night when the waiter asked for their orders. Adolph ordered bourbon and water. The last one on the list was Shive and since the others had ordered bourbon, the waiter asked Shive if he wanted the same. Shive said, "No, just bring me water. I had just as soon commit adultery as to drink that stuff."

Adolph immediately spoke up and said. "Wait a minute waiter - you didn't tell me I had a choice."

The results of that tournament were as follows:

August 3	Kentucky 67,	Warsaw University 58
August 4	Kentucky 104,	Cambridge University 45
August 6	Kentucky 91,	Salonika University 60
August 10	Kentucky 82,	Istanbul University 36
August 11	Kentucky 87,	Warsaw University 57

World's Championship Tournament. Total scores, UK 2950, Opponents 2284.

Before the team left for the Middle East, Pat Riley hurt his back while water skiing. During the Middle East tour, Pat reinjured his back while diving in the hotel pool. Adolph said later he hurt his back that day while "showing off in front of the girls."

The next day after the team returned to Lexington, Louie brought me a beautiful hand-made jewelry box inlaid with mother-of-pearl. Bless his heart, when he gave it to me he said, "Doc, you probably don't have any use for this box, but I just had to bring you something." Needless to say, I shall cherish that gift for the rest of my days.

In summary, this team, especially the five starters, operated so much like a well-oiled machine and exhibited the most perfect example of true synchronism of any basketball team I have ever seen. Such synchronized team work was the result of a complete dedication, determination and unselfishness on the part of every player plus superior coaching by our two great coaches.

Riley Royal Chocolate Cake

1 stick butter
4 tablespoons cocoa
1/2 cup oil
1 cup water
2 cups flour
2 cups sugar
1/2 cup buttermilk
2 eggs
1 teaspoon baking soda
1 teaspoon vanilla

Place butter, cocoa, oil and water in saucepan; bring to a boil. In large bowl, mix flour and sugar; stir in cocoa mixture. Add buttermilk, eggs, baking soda and vanilla; mix well. Bake at 350° 35 minutes for 2 layer pans, 45-50 minutes for bundt pan.
Cool on rack for 5 minutes; remove from pan. Cool thoroughly and frost.

Frosting:

1/2 stick butter
3 tablespoons milk
3 tablespoons cocoa
1/2 box sifted powdered sugar
1 teaspoon vanilla
1/2 cup nuts, chopped

Boil butter, milk and cocoa; add remaining ingredients and mix well.

Pat Riley

Cheese Wafers

2 cups flour
2 sticks butter or margarine
2 cups sharp cheddar cheese, shredded
2 cups Rice Krispies
1/4 teaspoon salt
1/8 teaspoon Cayenne pepper

Mix all ingredients and chill for at least 2 hours. Form
into small balls; place on a cookie sheet and press down
with a fork to flatten. Bake at 375° for about 15 minutes.

Tom Kron

Coach Rupp, Mrs. Rupp and Marie Jackson

Coach Rupp, Mrs. Rupp and Dr. Jackson

Jim Vick, Coach Rupp, Donna Vick, Mrs. Rupp

The Sorghum Festival at West Liberty, KY, October 1974

Dr. Jackson, Marie Jackson, Mrs. Rupp, Coach Rupp, 3/27/71

Dr. Jackson and cat's paws at U. K. football stadium

Alan Vick, Dr. V. A. Jackson and Steve Vick

Coach Rupp and Sparkle, our poodle

Dr. Jackson and Kevin Grivey, Tamworth, Australia

Dr. Jackson leading his famous yell with U.K. cheerleader

Adolph Rupp buried in Lexington after brief funeral rites

LEXINGTON, Ky. (AP) — Adolph Rupp, eulogized as a man who strove for excellence in all things, was buried Tuesday as many of his former players paid a final tribute to their coach.

Rupp, who in 42 years transformed the University of Kentucky's basketball program into a national power, was buried after a brief funeral service.

Rupp, 76, died Saturday night at the UK Medical Center, where he had been hospitalized since Nov. 9. He suffered more than a year from cancer of the spine, and was also plagued by diabetes and heart and kidney ailments.

Among the players on hand were representatives of each of Rupp's four NCAA champions — Wah Wah Jones and Ralph Beard from the 1948 and 1949 teams dubbed "The Fabulous Five"; Cliff Hagan and Frank Ramsey from the 1951 titleists; and Vernon Hatton, Adrian Smith and John Crigler from "The Fiddlin' Five" of 1958.

Dr. M. Glynn Burke, pastor of Central Christian Church where Rupp was a member, characterized college basketball's winningest coach as a man whose life "was a quest for excellence."

"He wanted to bring out the best in the game itself, the best in each of his players, the best in his teams. He wanted first-class performance and wasn't satisfied with anything less," Burke said.

"Of course, some of the coach's language did not exactly come from the Bible," Burke said, adding, "his mind was on basketball, even when

he could on occasion be heard to quote that familiar psalm, 'I will lift up mine eyes to the hills from whence does my help come,' but he was thinking of those hills in eastern Kentucky, where help came in the form of some big, strong players."

Those players to whom Burke referred helped Rupp win 874 games in 42 seasons, including the four NCAA titles, a National Invitation Tournament crown and 27 Southeastern Conference championships.

Also on hand for the services was Joe B. Hall, who played and coached under Rupp before replacing The Baron in 1972; Rupp's longtime assistant Harry C. Lancaster; Alabama Coach C.M. Newton, who played for Rupp's 1951 national champions; and Cincinnati Coach Gale Catlett, a former Rupp assistant.

Kentucky Gov. Julian M. Carroll, who declared Tuesday a day of mourning and ordered flags flown at half-staff across the state, also attended, as did University of Kentucky President Otis Singletary.

Rupp's wife, Esther, sat with the coach's son, Adolph Jr., his wife, and Rupp's two grandchildren.

After the service, the 10 pallbearers — including former Commissioner of Baseball A.B. "Happy" Chandler, Rupp's longtime friend — placed the walnut coffin into a black hearse. The procession to Lexington Cemetery wound past UK's Memorial Coliseum, the 11,500 seat facility where Rupp's teams played from 1950 until he was forced into retirement in 1972.

(AP Laserphoto)

Pallbearers at Rupp funeral; (clockwise) Gov. "Happy Chandler", John Ferguson, Doug Billips, Dr. Lyman Ginger, Dr. Jackson, John Y. Brown, Sr., Cecil Bell, Claude Vaughan and Robert Sparks (not shown)

Marie Jackson at Rupp Memorial

Chapter VIII

The 1966 - 68 UK team won 13 and lost 13.

From 32 - 2 to 13 - 13 certainly was a colossal come-down. However, there were unavoidable events that all but made this descent almost predictable.

Two of the main cogs in that great machine were lost by graduation. Larry Conley was the offensive quarterback who ran the team from his forward position. Tommy Kron was without question one of the greatest defensive guards of all time. Losing two-fifths of the team left such a void, it was almost impossible to rebuild in time to have another great season. But that is not the whole story.

Pat Riley's back injury seemed to gradually worsen during the off season. He was advised by the neurosurgeon that the trouble was a "slipped disc" that should be removed. However, Pat was afraid the operation might hinder his chances to play professional ball and decided against the surgery.

We realized soon after practice officially started in October 1966 that Pat's back was a troublesome problem. It required a lot of attention from both the trainer and team physician plus a lot of hard work, suffering and special exercise on Pat's part.

Although our win-loss record was quite poor, compared to all of Coach Rupp's other seasons at UK, it was a season of many interesting games and some disheartening ones. We lost all four of our overtime games, starting December 5, with Illinois in Lexington 98 to 97; January 5, to Vanderbilt 91 to 89 also at home; the bitterest of all, to Tennessee 52 to 50 in 2 OVERTIME, in Lexington; and finally to Mississippi State 77 to 72 in Lexington. But we had one "pro" type game I will never forget. We defeated Northwestern in Evanston 118 to 116, on December 10, 1966.

That game had a most interesting conflict between our two starting guards. We had a young guard, whose name was Bob Talent and he was an outstanding outside shooter. But Bob was a little jealous of Louie and, at times, was a little slow in passing the ball him. In this game, the ball was getting to Louie a split second after the defensive guard got to Louie and he had to rush his shots, resulting in missed shots. Adolph saw what was happening and called timeout with Northwestern leading by seven points. He quickly showed Bob what he was doing then said, "You are supposed to get that pass to Louie a split second before that guard gets in front of Louie and, by God, you had better get it there in time from now on." During the next two minutes, Louie made seven consecutive jump shots and we won 118 to 116. That one little change in strategy was just one more example where Adolph detected a flaw and immediately corrected it to win the game. He may not have been a coaching genius to some of his critics, but there has never been a better one.

The feeling Bob had for Louie did not improve too much, which was understandable because he had never played opposite such an outstanding guard before. It finally reached a climax in Knoxville against Tennessee, February 13, 1967. Bob was bringing the ball up the floor and instead of passing to Louie, he threw it unusually hard while Louie was not looking. The ball barely missed the side of Louie's head and went out of bounds. Adolph immediately benched Bob and, as the player walked by our bench, he said to the coach, "I don't give a damn if I never play for

Kentucky again."

Adolph said, "Don't worry; you won't." Bob quit the team the next day.

I was very fond of both guards and Bob's leaving really upset me. He was, and is, a wonderful person and was a very talented player. On February 18, just a week after Mississippi State had defeated UK in Lexington 77 to 72, we played them in Starkville just five days after the Knoxville game.

Well, it seems that unpleasant news travels fast. When our players took the floor that night, a group of State students had a cheering section near our bench. Their primary yell was "We want Talent - we want Talent." That chant, loud and clear, continued until we had the game well under control. Immediately after the game, I stood in front of that group and when they all got quiet, I yelled, "Have you had enough talent for one night?" We had just won 103 to 74. I was so elated, I called my brother Herschel in Clinton, Kentucky.

We were at Auburn Sunday, February 26 for the game there on Monday. During practice Sunday afternoon, Pat could not stoop over far enough to pick up the basketball and he actually had to squat to reach it.

When practicing Tuesday, February 28 for the Vanderbilt game to be held March 4, Pat was in so much pain I suggested to Adolph we put him in the hospital for a few days of traction and rest. We talked to Pat and he agreed to enter the hospital if I would be his doctor and he be permitted to come back each day and shoot free throws a few minutes. We agreed to Pat's requests and I took him to St. Joseph Hospital.

To show that these players are really just kids and how they grow attached to members of the coaching staff, while filling out the admission form, the nurse asked Pat who was his nearest relative that he wanted notified in case of emergency. Without any hesitation, he said, "Dr. V.A. Jackson."

Pat's stay in the hospital helped his back considerably but we still lost the Vanderbilt game 110 to 94.

After losing those three consecutive games the first two

weeks in January, then losing to Tennessee 52 to 50 in two over-times in Lexington, a man stopped me in a drug store the next day and wanted to know if I didn't think Coach Rupp had gotten too old to coach. I said, "Well, let's first look at his record. Last year his team won 32 games and lost 2 and he was voted the #1 bas-ketball coach in the nation. If your estimate of his age is correct, he sure aged pretty fast in a year. That was a pretty silly question."

After coming so close to a losing season in 1966 - 67 with a record of 13 wins and 13 losses, Coach Rupp had only five more seasons of coaching basketball at University of Kentucky. But during those five seasons, he refuted any claims or beliefs that he was too old to coach. The record shows that the 1967 - 68 UK team won 22 and lost 5. It won the UKIT and the SEC champi-onships. It lost to Ohio State 82 to 81 in the final game of the NCAA Mideast Regional in the last second of play.

In 1968 - 69, the team won 23, lost 5. They too won the UKIT and SEC championships, but lost to Marquette 81 to 74 in the NCAA Mideast Tournament at Madison, Wisconsin.

The 1969 -70 squad won 26 and lost 2. The lone regular season loss was to Vanderbilt in Nashville. Again, they won the UKIT and SEC championships, losing to Jacksonville 106 to 100 in the final game of the NCAA Mideast Tournament at Columbus, Ohio.

1970 - 71, the record shows 22 wins against 6 losses. They lost the final game to Purdue 89 to 83 in the UKIT but won the SEC Championship. Western Kentucky beat us 107 to 83 in the first game of the NCAA Mideast Regional Tournament in Athens, Georgia.

For this team, Coach Rupp recruited a seven footer - his only black player - Tom Payne. Tom played one year, 1970 - 71, and signed a pro-contract. Tom was a big disappointment although he had what many considered unlimited basketball potential. He was, without exception, physically the strongest col-lege basketball player I have ever seen. However, his final UK game was a disaster. We were heavy favorites in that game with Western Kentucky in the NCAA Mideast Regional, in Athens,

Georgia on March 18, 1971. But Western won 107 to 83. Payne got one rebound and played a very poor game. In fact, he stood around like a little dog in high oats, not knowing which way to go nor what to do when he got there.

That game was not only an embarrassing loss to the University but, it was a double disaster to Coach Rupp. He only had one more year before his retirement, and the loss of that game eliminated UK from the NCAA tournament.

Well, the next year, 1971 - 72, was Coach Rupp's last year as UK's Basketball Coach. He retired after that season, closing out 42 years of an excellent coaching career and one of the greatest in basketball history. He had won more college basketball games that any coach in history, 879 games including 4 NCAA Championships.

That year, 1971 - 72, UK won the UKIT and the SEC, and was ranked 14th nationally. In the NCAA Mideast Regional Tournament in Dayton, Ohio, UK defeated Marquette, which was ranked Number 5 nationally, 85 to 69. In Rupp's final game as the UK coach, we lost to Florida State 73 to 54. I sincerely think that game concluded the greatest college coaching career in the history of basketball.

Even though Coach Rupp's final season was a highly successful one, it was also one with melancholy feelings during the practice sessions. Knowing the condition of Rupp's health, especially his cardiovascular system, I definitely felt he was pushing himself more than he should. This seemed to be especially true when there were members of the media present.

Due to the above conditions, I was not in favor of extending Coach Rupp's contract for additional years and I so apprised Mrs. Rupp of my feelings since our two families had been unusually close friends for the last 20 years or so.

Chapter IX

During the 40 to 41 years Coach Rupp coached at the University of Kentucky, his teams won more basketball games than any coach in history; won more Southeastern Conference Championships than all the other Conference schools combined; and he had the highest winning percentage of any coach in history.

Coach Rupp was, however, much more than a basketball coach. His talents were many and diverse. He was an astute businessman, keeping abreast of the business world at all times, and was a prolific reader of the *Wall Street Journal*. He had a fantastic memory and followed the trends in the stock market daily.

Coach Rupp was an excellent farmer and was a highly successful cattle man. He kept a beautiful herd of white-face Hereford cattle. His cattle were sold by the head, not by the pound or hundredweight, and they sold for fancy prices.

Boy howdy, many was the time whent he would call me after church on Sunday to go with him to the farm. His farm was just over the Bourbon County line and was comprised of approximately 550 acres of beautiful bluegrass pasture land. He had a tobacco base for several thousand pounds and raised up to that limit of burley tobacco every year as well as a sizeable crop of corn, hay, and so forth.

Since I was raised on a farm in Hickman County, Kentucky, I thoroughly enjoyed those sojourns to the farm. It was such experiences together that helped to cement our friendship into such a lifelong one.

Adolph had so many quality talents that trying to write about all of them would be a clumsy effort, but one talent was so outstanding I would be remiss not mention it.

Coach Rupp was a fantastic public speaker. It was my good fortune and great privilege to be with him many times when he was a guest speaker. His speeches were all different, each one was most appropriate for that particular occasion and never did I see him have a written speech or use notes during his talks. He invariably sprinkled a few appropriate jokes as he went along but never did he tell a joke that might be embarrassing to the ladies in the audience. He was a real gentleman at all times.

Coach Rupp was far from being a loner. In fact, he very much disliked being alone.

Once in Louisville when we were getting ready to play Notre Dame, I was in the coffee shop eating a bowl of soup and as he passed by, Coach Rupp saw me. He came in and asked me to go to his room with him to dress for the game. While dressing, he put his shoes on before his pants, his usual procedure but this time he was going to wear a new brown suit and the pant legs were cut a little smaller than his older ones and would not go on over his shoes. Boy howdy. He called his tailor every kind of a name in the book for being so damn skimpy with the cloth and charging him three prices for such a suit.

Another time when he was a patient in the hospital and the team was to play in Florida and Georgia on January 15th and 17th, 1972, the day before the team left for Gainesville, he said to me, "Doc, I sure wish you would stay here and listen to those two games with me - then we can discuss both games here in my room." Needless to say, that broke my string of consecutive games without a miss. There was no way I was going to refuse his wish.

I want to share some interesting incidents that happened many years before I became Adolph's' personal physician. The facts are taken from Russell Rice's book ***Kentucky Basketball's Big Blue Machine***.

Coach Rupp's first game at UK was played with Georgetown college on December 18, 1930. Ellis Johnson scored the first field goal for Coach Rupp just after Harry Lancaster scored the first one for Georgetown against Rupp's team. Harry later became Adolph's assistant for 20 years, 1946 - 1966.

In January, 1987, I visited Mr. Cecil Bell and Mrs. Bell in their home in Fayette County. Cecil is now paralyzed as a result of a tractor accident. I mention this because Cecil told me during my visit that he played in that game against Georgetown. The final score was UK 67, Georgetown 19.

Cecil did not start the game but when he went in, he was told to guard Lancaster and to stop the SOB from scoring. Harry was high point man for the game with 16 points. After the game, Adolph called Cecil aside and asked, "Do you realize why Lancaster scored all those points against you?"

Cecil told me, "Doc, I was so scared, I could not say a word - I just stood there and shook. We were scared to death of him. He saw how scared I was and then he said, 'Aw hell. Don't let it bother you - you will do better next time. At least, you sure as hell better do better.'"

Cecil became one of Adolph's lifetime friends. We still enjoy reminiscing about him at every opportunity.

Rupp once told a group of writers that when a boy baby is born in Kentucky, the mother naturally wants him to follow in the footsteps of another Kentuckian, Abraham Lincoln and become president. If not president, she wants him to play basketball for the University of Kentucky.

Rupp was a tough disciplinarian and a task-master even during his early years at UK. During a game that UK won with Cincinnati in Alumni Gym in 1933, Jack Tingle missed four consecutive free throws. That was on Saturday night. At practice

Monday when the first drill started, Rupp called Jack over and said, "Get that chair and place it on the foul line and you sit there the rest of the afternoon and look at that goal." And he did. Tingle said later that his free throw shooting was quite good after that.

In 1936 the athletic director had suspended Joe (Red) Hagan but when the team left the next day for a game with Notre Dame, Red went and dressed for the game but was not allowed to play. In the first half, UK fell behind by 14 points. Rupp pulled a piece of paper from his pocket, waved it to Red and said, "I just got a telegram. Your suspension has been lifted and you can go in now." Hagan went in and scored 12 points but UK still lost the game.

Two years before Coach Rupp went to UK, he became the high school basketball coach at Freeport, Illinois, after coaching wrestling at Marshalltown High School in Iowa the year before. During his two years at Freeport, his teams won 66 games and lost 17.

Adolph used to say that many times while coaching at Freeport he went to Madison to see Wisconsin play basketball. Dr. Walter Meanwell was a very successful coach at Wisconsin and Adolph said he learned a lot from him. When I was in high school, I also learned about Dr. Meanwell and ordered his book on coaching basketball. Our team at Clinton High School copied four basic plays from that book which helped us to a 17 - 4 season.

It was the guest speaker at Freeport's basketball banquet in 1930, Craig Ruby, who told Adolph about the coaching job vacancy at Kentucky.

Adolph said that when he went to Lexington for his interview, he was late arriving for lunch at McVey Hall and all he had to eat was one piece of cold fish. He said, "I was not impressed with Lexington."

The UK officials offered Adolph the same salary he was making at Freeport but since it afforded him an opportunity to break into college coaching, he accepted.

My good friend, Aggie Sale once said, "My first impressions of our new coach were that I saw in him a man of intelligence, great leadership, personality, and all the other splendid qualities he has shown down through the years." Aggie and I became close friends during Adolph's first two years at UK.

Once when trying to defend his spending so much practice time on defense, Rupp said, "Fans don't appreciate good defensive players but you must have them. It's just like on a farm; fertilizer must be spread. Nobody likes to spread the stuff, but it has to be done. A lot of boys just want to shoot but, you have to have defense."

Before UK's away game with Chicago in December 1932, Frenchy DeMoisey asked sports writers "What's the scoring record for this gym?"

"Twenty-four points," was the reply. "Why?"

"Because I'm going to break it." UK won 58 to 26 but when Frenchy scored his 24th point, Rupp took him out then said, "I wasn't worried about Frenchy breaking any records. I was just concerned that Chicago scored so many points."

The popularity of Rupp's basketball team was clearly evident at the next home game with Ohio State.

A mob formed in front of Alumni Gym entrance, making it impossible for ticket holders to enter. Several people received minor injuries, and the danger was heightened by boys attempting to climb through the transoms. A woman was knocked down inside the building and the second half was delayed five minutes while the crowd was cleared from the playing floor. Later the problem was partially solved by roping off that part of the street in front of the gym and assigning football players to keep order. Students would be admitted through basement doors, and all doors would be closed after a capacity crowd was admitted. The need for a new fieldhouse was evident.

In January, 1934, basketball was not as popular as it is today. As a result, even though UK had run its two-season victory string to 17, by the end of that month attendance had steadily declined, due mostly to the fact that football was the main topic of conversation.

Vernon Hatton, one of UK's class All-Americans likes to tell about Rupp's tenet for being punctual. In his book, Vernon says, "The coach insisted that players be on time for every appointment and 10:00 really meant to be there at 9:30. The wise players would always be a little early - in the lobby a little early to go to the arena - dressed a little bit early for the game - at the bus a little early for the airport, etc. Therefore we were never, never late." However, there is usually an exception to most rules.

Once we were playing at Starkville, Mississippi and our All-American forward was a few seconds late getting on the bus and he was preceded a few steps by the non-All-American forward. Well, the "lesser" forward really caught hell for being late and causing the "other guy" to be late.

Rupp was once heard to say in answer to a criticism about his aloofness to his players, "If I wanted to be a father to all of you boys, I would have adopted 20 boys and moved to the farm and raised white-faced cattle. It is none of my business if your girlfriend left you. I don't want your personal problems. So, get out there and play basketball."

I happen to know that this was not Adolph's true feelings but he wanted the players to think it was. One player told me a few years after graduating from UK, "Doctor, at times he makes you so mad you actually hate him and you think, you old son-of-a-bitch, I'll show you I can play basketball and you go out there and play your heart out." That was just one of Adolph's psychological ploys he used so many, many times to wring the last drop of basketball from a player and actually make him play better that the player ever thought he could. Rupp's good players played like great ones and his great players were super.

Adolph Rupp died December 10, 1977.

Whatta loss. He will be long remembered - but, never replaced.

First place winners on cruise ship for costume competition, Dr. Jackson and Marie Jackson as basketball player and cheerleader.

Dr. Jackson, Sam Bowie and our grandson, Alan Vick

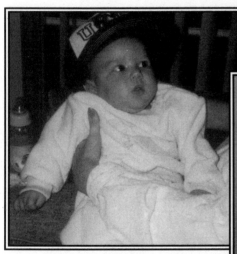

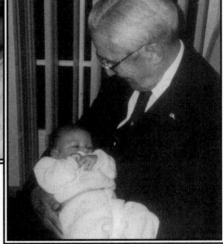

*Dylan Vick - Dr. Jackson's great
grandson with U.K. cap*

*Dr. Jackson holding great grandson,
Dylan Vick*

Dr. Jackson and grandson, Alan Vick discussing 1994 game

Dr. Jackson and Mike Phillips

*Dr. Jackson celebrating his 75th birthday in St. Louis
when we won the N.C.A.A. in 1978*

*Dr. Jackson and President
of U.K., Otis Singletary*

Dr. Jackson and Governor A. B. "Happy" Chandler

*Coach Rupp and
Marie Jackson
during his illness*

Hot Chicken Salad

2 cups chicken, cooked and diced
1 cup celery, diced
1/2 cup almonds, slivered
1/2 teaspoon salt, optional
1/2 teaspoon onion, grated
2 tablespoons lemon juice
1 cup mayonnaise
3/4 cup cheddar cheese, shredded
2/3 cup potato chips, crushed

Heat oven to 375°. Mix all ingredients, except cheese and chips. Pour into a greased oblong baking dish. Combine cheese and chips; sprinkle over top of casserole. Bake 20 minutes.
Serves 4.

Russell Rice

Angel Food Cake

1-1/4 cups cake flour
1/2 cup sugar
1-1/2 cups egg whites
1/4 teaspoon salt
1-1/4 teaspoons cream of tartar
1-1/3 cups sugar
1 teaspoon vanilla
1/4 teaspoon almond extract

Sift cake flour and sugar together four times; set aside. In a very large bowl beat egg whites and salt, by hand, until foamy. Add cream of tartar and beat until very stiff. Add 1-1/3 cups of sugar, 2 tablespoons at a time; beat well after each addition. Add vanilla and almond extract. Fold in flour, 4 tablespoons at a time. Bake in angel food mold or tube pan at 350° for 35 minutes. Remove from oven; invert on plate to cool.

Angel Food Icing

2 cups sugar
1/2 cup water
1/8 teaspoon cream of tartar
2 egg whites
1/2 teaspoon vanilla
1/4 teaspoon almond extract

Cook sugar, water and cream of tartar until soft ball stage. Beat egg whites with mixer until stiff; add syrup very slowly, beating all the time. When all syrup has been beaten into egg whites, add vanilla and almond extract. When icing stands in peaks again, it is ready for frosting the cake.

Cecil Bell

Baked Stuffed Zucchini

8 small zucchini
2 medium onions, chopped
1 clove garlic, chopped
12 sprigs parsley, chopped
3 tablespoons olive oil
1 cup spinach
1 teaspoon oregano
1-1/2 teaspoons salt
1/4 teaspoon pepper
1/2 cup Parmesan cheese
3 eggs, beaten
2/3 cup dry bread crumbs

Cook zucchini 5 minutes in boiling water; drain, cool and cut in half. Scoop out pulp and save, leaving 1/4" around shell. Sauté onions, garlic and parsley in oil. Put zucchini pulp and spinach in blender and mix. Drain off excess liquid and add to onion mixture. Sauté 3 minutes; add seasonings, cheese and eggs. Sprinkle zucchini shells lightly with salt; fill with mixture and sprinkle with bread crumbs. Place in a casserole dish and cover. Bake for 20 minutes at 350°. Uncover and bake 10 minutes longer. Serves 6 to 8.

Scotty Baesler

Coffee Cake

1/4 cup sugar
1/4 cup brown sugar, packed
1/2 cup nuts, chopped
1 teaspoon cinnamon
3 ounce package instant lemon pudding mix
1 yellow cake mix
8 ounces sour cream
1/2 cup oil
4 eggs
1 teaspoon vanilla

Mix sugar, brown sugar, nuts and cinnamon and set aside. Preheat oven to 350°. In large bowl combine pudding mix, cake mix, sour cream, oil, eggs and vanilla. Beat well for about 5 minutes. Grease and flour bundt pan. Layer 1/3 of batter, sprinkle on 1/3 cup topping. Repeat layers ending with topping. Bake for 45-55 minutes or until done. Cool completely.

This coffee cake freezes beautifully.

Dwane Casey

Baked Lasagna

1/4 cup salad oil
1/2 cup onion, diced
2 cloves garlic, minced
1/2 pound ground beef
1 tablespoon basil
3 tablespoons parsley
1 teaspoon salt
1/4 teaspoon pepper
14-ounce can tomatoes
6-ounce can tomato paste
1 pound lasagna noodles
6 quarts boiling water, with 1 tablespoon salt
1 tablespoon olive oil
1 pound mozzarella cheese
12 ounces cottage cheese
2-1/2-ounce jar Parmesan cheese

Brown onion and garlic in salad oil. Brown meat and combine with onion and garlic. Add parsley, basil, salt, pepper, tomatoes and tomato paste. Cover and simmer 40 minutes; pour off excess grease. Cook noodles for 15 minutes in salted boiling water to which olive oil has been added. Drain, cover with cold water and drain again. In a 9x12" pan, put layer of sauce, layer of noodles, layer of mozzarella cheese and cottage cheese, repeat layers. Top with Parmesan cheese. Bake covered at 350° for 15 minutes. Remove cover and bake an additional 5 minutes.

Can be frozen and cooked later, about 1 hour.

Russ Cochran

Pat's Pound Cake

2 sticks butter (not margarine)
1/2 cup shortening
3 cups sugar
5 eggs
3 cups cake flour
1 cup milk
1 teaspoon vanilla
1 teaspoon lemon extract
1/2 teaspoon baking powder

Have all ingredients at room temperature before beginning. Cream butter and shortening. Add sugar, then eggs, one at a time, mixing thoroughly with each addition. Add flour and milk gradually, always beginning and ending with flour. Add vanilla, lemon extract and baking powder; mix well. Pour into a well greased and floured bundt pan. Do not preheat oven. Begin cooking cake in a cold oven. Bake for 1 hour and 15 minutes at 350°. Watch cake carefully in order to not overbake or it will become dry.

Pat Doyle

Old Kentucky Jam Cake

1/2 cup butter
2 cups sugar
2 eggs
1 teaspoon each cloves, cinnamon, allspice and cocoa
2 teaspoons soda
4 cups flour
2 cups sour milk
1 cup blackberry jam

Cream butter and add sugar; beat well. Add eggs and beat for 5 minutes. Sift dry ingredients together at least twice. Add dry ingredients and milk to batter, beating well. Add jam. Place in 3 layer cake pans which have been greased and floured. Bake at 325° for 30 minutes. Frost with caramel icing if desired.

Doug Flynn

Chinese Beef
with Broccoli and Snow Peas

1 pound beef sirloin steak, cut 1/2" thick
4 teaspoons cornstarch
2 tablespoons soy sauce
2 teaspoons cooking oil
1 pound fresh broccoli or
2 10-ounce packages frozen
1 pound fresh snow peas or
2 10-ounce packages frozen
1 ginger root, thinly sliced or
1/2 teaspoon ground ginger
3 tablespoons cooking oil
2 green onion with tops, sliced thin
Cooked rice

Slice beef diagonally in 3" strips. Combine cornstarch, soy sauce and 2 teaspoons oil in bowl. Add beef; toss to coat well. Slice broccoli lengthwise in thin strips, 3" long. Heat ginger in 3 tablespoons oil in electric wok or skillet at 375°, Add broccoli and snow peas, stir fry 3 to 5 minutes. Remove from pan. Add more oil if necessary; stir fry beef until well browned, about 5 minutes. Return broccoli and snow peas to pan; add 1/2 cup water. Cook and stir until gravy thickens. Garnish with onions. Serve over rice.
Serves 4.

Ralph Hacker

Manicotti

Sauce:

1 pound hot Italian sausage, cut into 2" pieces
1/2 pound lean ground beef
29-ounce can tomato puree or plum tomatoes
6-ounce can tomato paste
1/2 teaspoon fennel
1/2 teaspoon oregano
1/2 teaspoon sweet basil
1/2 teaspoon parsley
1 bay leaf
2 cloves garlic, chopped
1/4 large onion, chopped
Small amount of crushed red pepper, optional
1/2 pound pepperoni, sliced

Brown sausage and ground beef in about 1 tablespoon of cooking oil. Add all other ingredients and simmer for 4 to 5 hours. Chicken can be added to sauce, boil until tender and remove from bone.

Manicotti stuffing

16 ounces Ricotta cheese
1/2 cup grated Romano cheese
4 ounces Provolone
1/4 cup parsley, chopped
1-1/2 teaspoons salt
1-1/2 teaspoons pepper
2 eggs, beaten

Combine all ingredients; stuff into manicotti shells which have been prepared according to package directions. Arrange in shallow pan and pour sauce over top. Bake at 375° for 20 minutes.

Jerry Hale

Vanilla Ice Cream
1 Gallon Freezer

4 egg yolks
3 cups sugar
2 tablespoons flour
Small pinch of salt
2-1/2 cups milk
1 package plain Knox gelatin
3/4 can evaporated milk
1 pint whipping cream
3 tablespoons vanilla

Beat egg yolks with a fork. Mix sugar, flour and salt together; add milk and eggs. Cook, stirring constantly, until mixture forms a custard of creamy consistency . Remove from stove and cool somewhat. Mix gelatin and 1/2 cup water and add to custard. Strain the mixture into another container to remove lumps. Cool. Mix in evaporated milk, whipping cream and vanilla; pour into freezer container. Add a layer of coarse salt and ice and turn crank, keep repeating adding salt and ice until crank become hard to turn. Remove the paddle and pack in additional ice, but be sure to cover the hole on top with paper napkins and plastic wrap. Let stand for 1/2 hour for the ice cream to harden.

If using fruit, you may follow the above ingredients but cut down on the vanilla.

Bill Keightley

Broccoli-Chicken Casserole

3 cups chicken, cooked and cut up
1/4 teaspoon curry powder
2 cans chicken soup
1 cup mayonnaise
2 packages frozen broccoli, cooked and drained
1 cup cheddar cheese, grated
1 cup bread or cracker crumbs
2 tablespoons butter

Mix chicken, curry powder, soup and mayonnaise. Place broccoli into a greased casserole. Pour chicken mixture over top of broccoli. Mix cheese, bread crumbs and butter; sprinkle on top of casserole. Bake at 350° until bubbly.

Jim LeMaster

French Onion Beef Au Jus

1/2 cup soy sauce
2 tablespoons oil
1 clove garlic, minced
1-1/2 teaspoons browning sauce
1 teaspoon Beau Monde seasoning
1-1/4 ounce package dry onion soup mix
5 cups water
3-1/2 pounds fresh beef brisket, trimmed of fat
2 large sweet onions, cut into 1/4" slices and separated into rings
1/4 cup butter
2 cups water
4 French rolls, sliced lengthwise and buttered
Grated Gruyere or Swiss cheese

Combine soy sauce, oil, garlic, browning sauce and Beau Monde seasoning in blender; blend on medium until smooth. Add onion soup mix and 5 cups water; blend on low until just mixed. Place brisket in 3-1/2 to 4 quart baking casserole or Dutch oven; pour soy sauce mixture over beef. Cover tightly and cook in 350° oven for 2 hours. Meanwhile, lightly brown onion rings in butter; add to beef. Continue cooking, covered, 1 hour or until beef is tender. Remove brisket from cooking liquid and let stand 20 minutes before carving. Add 2 cups water to cooking liquid, keep hot. Carve brisket across the grain, into 1/4" slices. Return slices to cooking liquid. Toast roll halves in broiler. To serve, place hot beef slices and liquid on top of rolls. Sprinkle with cheese and broil just until cheese melts.
Serves 8.

Larry Lentz

Mom's Potato Salad

6 to 8 medium size potatoes,
boiled with skin on, peeled and diced
2 medium onions, chopped
1 tablespoon celery seed
1 large carrot, peeled and grated
4 to 6 hard boiled eggs, peeled and chopped
1-1/2 cups Miracle Whip salad dressing
1/2 cup sour cream
2 tablespoons salad mustard
2 tablespoons sugar
1 teaspoon salt
Small amount of cream

In large bowl combine potatoes, onion, celery seed, carrot and hard boiled eggs. In medium bowl combine remaining ingredients; pour over potato mixture and blend together. Best if made the day before serving. Serve cold.

Kyle Macy

Lemon Pudding Cake

3/4 cup sugar
2 tablespoons cornstarch
3 tablespoons melted butter
1 teaspoon grated lemon rind
1/4 cup lemon juice
1/2 cup milk
3 egg yolks, well beaten
3 egg whites, stiffly beaten

Mix first 7 ingredients; fold in egg whites. Pour in 8" square pan. Place pan in a larger pan on oven rack. Pour in hot water to 1" in larger pan. Bake at 350° for 1 hour. Serve warm. The longer it cooks, the more cake-like. A warm lemon gravy is spooned on cake from the bottom of the pan.

Keith Madison

My Mother's Chocolate Cake

5-1/2 squares of unsweetened chocolate
1 cup hot water
1 cup butter
2 cups brown sugar
1-1/2 cups sugar
4 eggs, separated
5 cups cake flour
2 teaspoons baking soda
2 teaspoons baking powder
1/2 teaspoon salt
2 cups buttermilk
2 teaspoons vanilla

Melt chocolate in water, set aside. Cream butter, brown sugar and sugar together; add yolks and mix well. Sift flour, soda, baking powder and salt together; add to creamed mixture alternately with buttermilk. Blend in vanilla and melted chocolate. Beat egg whites until stiff; carefully fold into cake batter. Pour into 3 layer cake pans which have been greased and floured. Bake at 325° for 20 minutes; turn up oven to 350° and bake for an additional 10 minutes.

You may half the recipe for 2 layers.

Icing:

2 tablespoons butter
2 squares chocolate
Powdered sugar
1 teaspoon vanilla

Melt butter and chocolate. Add powdered sugar until right consistency. Add vanilla. May add a little water if necessary.

C. M. Newton

Blueberry Salad or Dessert

2 packages blueberry or blackberry gelatin
1 can blueberries, drained, reserving juice
Small can crushed pineapple, drained, reserving juice
1 cup sour cream
8 ounce package cream cheese
1/2 cup sugar
1-1/2 teaspoons vanilla
1/2 cup nuts, chopped

Dissolve gelatin in 2 cups boiling water. Add fruit and 1 cup of juice drained from pineapple and blueberries. Let congeal. Blend remaining ingredients, except nuts, and spread on top of gelatin a few hours before serving. Sprinkle nuts on top.
Serves 10 to 12.

Mike Phillips

Robey Red Beans

1 bag dried beans
1 pound ham pieces
1 pound smoked sausage
2-3 large white onions, minced
1 clove garlic, minced
Bacon drippings
3 beef bouillon cubes
3 bay leaves
Cooked rice

Wash and sort red beans. Cube ham and slice sausage. In a large, heavy iron pot with bacon drippings, cook ham pieces until red and edges begin to brown. Set ham aside. Brown sausage in same pot and set aside. Add onions and garlic and cook until transparent, turning often and scraping bottom of pot to loosen all remnants of ham and sausage. Return meat to pot and add about 1/2 to 3/4 gallon of water, depending on the thickness you desire. Add bouillon cubes and bay leaves; let come to a boil and reduce heat. Cover and cook about 45 minutes. Additional water may be needed. Cook until beans are tender and soft. Serve over cooked rice. Red beans need a lot of cooking time — almost all day. If you like it spicy, add a dash or 2 of hot sauce before digging in.

Rick Robey

Strawberry Cream Squares

6-ounce package strawberry gelatin
2 cups boiling water
2 10-ounce packages frozen strawberries
13-1/2-ounce can crushed pineapple
2 large ripe bananas, finely diced
1 cup sour cream

Dissolve gelatin in boiling water. Add strawberries, stirring until thawed. Pour half of mixture into 9x13 dish. Add pineapple and bananas. Spread evenly with sour cream. Pour remaining gelatin mixture over the top. Chill until firm. Cut into 9 squares. Top with sour cream dollops.
Serves 9.

Chip Rupp

Corn-Squash Casserole

1 pound fresh summer squash (4 - 6)
Salt, pepper and butter to taste
1/4 cup cream
3 tablespoons sugar
1 egg, slightly beaten
1 cup fresh corn
1 cup cracker crumbs
1/4 cup butter, melted
Dash seasoned salt and pepper
1/4 cup Parmesan cheese

Cook squash until tender; add salt, pepper and butter. Mash squash and add cream, sugar and egg. Mix in corn. Place in casserole dish. Mix together cracker crumbs, butter, seasoned salt, pepper and Parmesan cheese. Sprinkle over casserole; bake at 400° until topping is brown.

Dr. Otis Singletary

Brown Sugar Pie

1/2 cup cream
2 cups brown sugar
3 eggs, beaten
1/2 cup butter, melted

Mix cream, sugar and eggs until well blended. Add cooled butter and beat in well. Pour into nine inch unbaked pie shell and bake at 350° until browned and shakes like jelly.

Larry Stamper

Beyond the Baron

Mail to:
McClanahan Publishing House, Inc.
P. O. Box 100
Kuttawa, KY 42055

For Orders call TOLL FREE
1-800-544-6959
Visa & MasterCard accepted

Please send me _____ copies of

Beyond the Baron	@$18.95 each	_____
Postage & handling		$ 3.50
Kentucky residents add 6% sales tax @$ 1.14 each		_____
Total enclosed		_____

Make check payable to McClanahan Publishing House

Ship to:
NAME

_____

ADDRESS

_____

CITY _____ STATE _____ZIP_____